READER'S GUIDE

TO

NARRATIVE OF THE
LIFE OF FREDERICK DOUGLASS,

AN AMERICAN SLAVE

READER'S GUIDE

TO

NARRATIVE OF THE LIFE OF FREDERICK DOUGLASS, AN AMERICAN SLAVE

Selected and Edited by

Joseph Coulson

Mike Levine

and

Steve Hettleman
Department of English, Redwood High School
Larkspur, California

Published by the Great Books Foundation
A nonprofit educational organization

Published and distributed by

The Great Books Foundation
A nonprofit educational organization

35 East Wacker Drive, Suite 2300
Chicago, IL 60601-2298
www.greatbooks.org

First printing
9 8 7 6 5 4 3 2 1

♾ This paper meets the requirements of
ANSI/NISO Z39.48-1992 (Permanence of Paper).

Library of Congress Cataloging-in-Publication Data

Reader's guide to Narrative of the life of Frederick Douglass, an American slave / selected and
edited by Joseph Coulson, Mike Levine, and Steve Hettleman.
        p. cm.
    Includes bibliographical references (p. 142).
    ISBN 1-880323-92-3 (alk. paper)
      1. Douglass, Frederick, 1818-1895. Narrative of the life of Frederick Douglass, an American
slave. 2. Abolitionists—United States—Biography—Study and teaching. 3. African American abolitionists—Biography—Study and teaching. 4. Slaves—United States—Biography—Study and teaching. 5. Slavery—United States—History—Sources. I. Coulson, Joseph. II. Levine, Mike. III.
Hettleman, Steve. IV. Great Books Foundation (U.S.)

E449.D749 2004
973.8'092—dc22

                                                                                              2004043244

Book cover and interior design:
William Seabright & Associates

About the Great Books Foundation

What is the Great Books Foundation?

The Great Books Foundation is an independent, nonprofit educational organization whose mission is to help people learn how to think and share ideas. Toward this end, the Foundation offers workshops in shared inquiry discussion and publishes collections of classic and modern texts for both children and adults.

  The Great Books Foundation was established in 1947 to promote liberal education for the general public. In 1962, the Foundation extended its mission to children with the introduction of Junior Great Books. Since its inception, the Foundation has helped thousands of people throughout the United States and in other countries begin their own discussion groups in schools, libraries, and community centers. Today, Foundation instructors conduct hundreds of workshops each year, in which educators and parents learn to lead shared inquiry discussion.

What resources are available to support my participation in shared inquiry?

The Great Books Foundation offers workshops in shared inquiry to help people get the most from discussion. Participants learn how to read actively, pose fruitful questions, and listen and respond to others effectively in discussion. All participants also practice leading a discussion and have an opportunity to reflect on the process with others. For more information about Great Books materials or workshops, call the Great Books Foundation at 1-800-222-5870 or visit our Web site at www.greatbooks.org.

Contents

Introduction

Published in 1845, Frederick Douglass's autobiography *Narrative of the Life of Frederick Douglass, an American Slave, Written by Himself* struck a blow against slavery not only because of what it said, but also because of what it was. The physical and psychological brutalities of slavery, and the perverse culture that sustained it, are vividly described in Douglass's narrative. But the fact that the book was written by a slave—that Douglass had managed to learn to read and write despite formidable obstacles and had penned a powerful indictment of the system that had tried to keep him illiterate—was undeniable evidence that slaves were as human as those who had to deny them their humanity in order to hold them in bondage.

In addition to its historical significance, Douglass's *Narrative* is an enduring work of literature: it confronts, and forces its readers to confront, questions that have challenged the world's greatest writers. What are the origins of moral and immoral behavior? What separates us from animals and makes us human? What values are worth dying for? Because the circumstances of his birth gave him no more legal standing than a piece of property until he escaped to freedom, Douglass brings a unique perspective to these questions.

This Reader's Guide to Douglass's *Narrative* is intended to deepen your engagement with the book in several ways. Discussion questions for the whole book and for each chapter help you focus on some of the complex issues the book raises and the moments at which it invites a variety of interpretations. The passages for close reading offer an opportunity for a more detailed exploration of Douglass's themes and techniques, while the suggestions for writing ask you to elaborate your responses to different aspects of the book. The selection of related materials expands the perspectives from which to consider Douglass and the *Narrative*. The voices that make up this section of the Reader's Guide condemn slavery, defend it, sing of its miseries, call for indiscriminate violence, and promote peaceful rebellion.

Douglass's *Narrative* is a provocative book. The Reader's Guide should enrich your thinking, discussion, and writing about the extraordinary story it tells.

About Shared Inquiry

Shared inquiry is the effort to achieve a more thorough understanding of a text by discussing questions, responses, and insights with others. For both the leader and the participants, careful listening is essential. The leader guides the discussion by asking questions about specific ideas and problems of meaning in the text, but does not seek to impose his or her own interpretation on the group.

During a shared inquiry discussion, group members consider a number of possible ideas and weigh the evidence for each. Ideas that are entertained and then refined or abandoned are not thought of as mistakes, but as valuable parts of the thinking process. Group members gain experience in communicating complex ideas and in supporting, testing, and expanding their thoughts. Everyone in the group contributes to the discussion, and while participants may disagree with each other, they treat each other's ideas respectfully.

This process of communal discovery is vital to developing an understanding of important texts and ideas, rather than merely cataloging knowledge about them. By reading and thinking together about important works, you and the other members of your group are joining a great conversation that extends across the centuries.

Guidelines for leading and participating in discussion

Over the past fifty years, the Great Books Foundation has developed guidelines that distill the experience of many discussion groups, with participants of all ages. We have found that when groups follow the procedures outlined below, discussions are most focused and fruitful.

1. **Read the selection before participating in the discussion.** This ensures that all participants are equally prepared to talk about the ideas in the work, and helps prevent talk that would distract the group from its purpose.

2. **Support your ideas with evidence from the text.** This keeps the discussion focused on understanding the selection and enables the group to weigh textual support for different answers and to choose intelligently among them.

3. **Discuss the ideas in the selection, and try to understand them fully before exploring issues that go beyond the selection.** Reflecting on a range of ideas and the evidence to support them makes the exploration of related issues more productive.

4. **Listen to others and respond to them directly.** Shared inquiry is about the give-and-take of ideas, a willingness to listen to others and to talk to them respectfully. Directing your comments and questions to other group members, not always to the leader, will make the discussion livelier and more dynamic.

5. **Expect the leader to ask questions, rather than answer them.** The leader is a kind of chief learner, whose role is to keep discussion effective and interesting by listening and asking questions. The leader's goal is to help the participants develop their own ideas, with everyone (the leader included) gaining a new understanding in the process. When participants hang back and wait for the leader to suggest answers, discussion falters.

How to make discussions more effective

- **Ask questions when something is unclear.** Simply asking someone to explain what he or she means by a particular word, or to repeat a comment, can give everyone in the group time to think about the idea in depth.

- **Ask for evidence.** Asking "What in the text gave you that idea?" helps everyone better understand the reasoning behind an answer, and it allows the group to consider which ideas have the best support.

- **Ask for agreement and disagreement.** "Does your idea agree with hers, or is it different?" Questions of this kind help the group understand how ideas are related or distinct.

- **Reflect on discussion afterward**. Sharing comments about how the discussion went and ideas for improvement can make each discussion better than the last.

Room arrangement and group size

Ideally, everyone in a discussion should be able to see and hear everyone else. When it isn't possible to arrange the seating in a circle or horseshoe, encourage group members to look at the person talking, acknowledging one another and not just the leader.

In general, shared inquiry discussion is most effective in groups of ten to twenty participants. If a group is much bigger than twenty, it is important to ensure that everyone has a chance to speak. This can be accomplished either by dividing the group in half for discussion or by setting aside time at the end of discussion to go around the room and give each person a chance to make a brief final comment.

❧

Using the Reader's Guide

"What to the Slave Is the Fourth of July?" by Frederick Douglass

"What to the Slave Is the Fourth of July?" a speech delivered by Douglass on July 5, 1852, will broaden students' study of Douglass and the *Narrative*. Perhaps Douglass's best-known speech, it shows how he used different literary and rhetorical techniques to suit his specific purposes as well as the expectations of the audience he was addressing. Discussing the speech either before or after reading the *Narrative* provides an excellent opportunity for comparative analysis.

Interpretive Questions for Discussion of *Narrative of the Life of Frederick Douglass*

Discussion gives participants of all ages an opportunity to express their ideas, listen to the perspectives of others, and synthesize different viewpoints to reach a deeper, more informed understanding of the *Narrative*. Effective questions help participants talk specifically about the content and language of the book, arrange details in logical order, and support their ideas with evidence from the text and personal experience.

Passages and Questions for Close Reading

Passages from the *Narrative* and related questions can be discussed in large and small groups or can be used for individual study and written response. The questions ask the reader to analyze specific themes, techniques, and terms as part of the interpretive process.

All readers will benefit from the challenges these questions pose. *Students in honors courses or courses qualifying for college credit will find these questions useful for exam preparation.*

Suggestions for Writing

Postdiscussion writing gives students the opportunity to consider new ideas and measure them against their personal experience and opinions. In these extended writing pieces, students can return to questions not fully resolved in discussion or investigate unexplored avenues of inquiry. Because thorough discussion requires such extensive engagement with the book, students are better prepared to present their ideas clearly and persuasively or, in the more creative writing assignments, to produce a more fully imagined response.

Background and Context

These selections will give readers a better sense of the world about which Douglass wrote. The description of a slave auction and the group of slave songs, for example, illuminate significant elements of the everyday life of a slave. The selections from Harriet A. Jacobs's autobiography and Nat Turner's confession enable readers to compare Douglass's voice with the voices of other slaves. Various attitudes toward slavery are represented by abolitionists as well as the apologist George Fitzhugh. Other selections offer additional perspectives on Douglass as both a writer and a public figure.

When used in the classroom, these selections invite teachers and students in English and history to join forces in discussion of the *Narrative,* examining the social, cultural, and political climate from which the book emerged.

Footnotes by the author are not bracketed; footnotes by the Great Books Foundation, an editor, or a translator are [bracketed].

Spelling and punctuation have been modernized and slightly altered for clarity, except for those passages reprinted from the Narrative.

NARRATIVE OF THE
LIFE OF FREDERICK DOUGLASS,

AN AMERICAN SLAVE

ABOUT THE AUTHOR

rederick Douglass was born Frederick Augustus Washington Bailey in February 1818 in Tuckahoe, on Maryland's Eastern Shore. His mother, Harriet Bailey, was a slave; his father was a white man, rumored to be his master, Aaron Anthony. Though born a slave, Douglass became one of the most important and influential African American leaders of the nineteenth century, a noted author, orator, and human rights advocate whose brilliant and powerful command of language brought him international recognition.

Douglass spent the first several years of his life in the care of his maternal grandmother, whose job was to raise slave children too young to work in the field. He saw his mother only a handful of times; she died when Douglass was seven. At the age of eight, Douglass was sent to Baltimore to work as a servant for Hugh and Sophia Auld, relatives of his master. It was a turning point in his life. As Douglass notes in his *Narrative*, "Going to live at Baltimore laid the foundation, and opened the gateway, to all my subsequent prosperity."

In Baltimore, Sophia Auld taught Douglass the alphabet and had moved on to helping him learn to spell three- and four-letter words. But her husband discovered her activities and angrily forbade her to continue. Douglass refused to be thwarted and pursued his own education in reading and writing, secretly and successfully. When he was about twelve years old, he bought a copy of *The Columbian Orator*, a compilation of speeches that gave voice to his thoughts against slavery, convinced him of the power of truth, and imbued him with a firm belief in the importance of human rights. This popular schoolbook

Negros ages as follows

old	Sarah was Born Sept. — — — — — —	1765	died Feby 1804
old	Henry Baly was Born May — — — — —	1767	died —
old	Betto was Born May — — — —	1774	Died — 1849
	Cate daughter of Sarah Born augst —	1789	
	Milly daughter of Betto Born Jany 28 — —	1790	
	Harriott daughter of Betto Born Feby 22 — —	1792	died
	Ham sun of Sarah Born March 6 —	1795	died 1814
	Noah sun of Sarah Born June — —	1799	
	Jinny daughter of Betto Born octr 28 —	1799	
Yong	Betto daughter of Betto Born octr 19 — —	1801	
	Avery wind daughter of Sarah Born March 22	1802	
Yong	Sarah daughter of Betto Born Feby —	1804	died 1816
	Marary daughter of Cate Born octr 29 —	1805	at Williamsn
	Bill sun of Milly Born June 7 —	1806	died 1813
	Maryann daughter of Betto Born apr 27	1806	
	Stephen sun of Betto Born apr 2 —	1808	died 1816
	Easter daughter of Betto Born augt —	1810	
	Betto farmer daughter of Milly Born Feby	1811	
	Augustos sun of Betto Born July	1812	died 1816
	Margret daughter of Milly Born Decr 10	1812	died 1815
	Perry sun of Harriott Born Jany — —	1813	
	Perry sun of Cate Born apl —	1813	
	Sarah daughter Harriott Born augt —	1814	
Yong	Ham sun of Milly Born Sept 21	1814	
	Cate daughter of Betto Born Jany —	1815	died 1815
	Phill son of Cate Born apl	1815	
	Eliza daughter of Harriott Born march	1816	
	Prissey daughter of Betto Born augt 15	1816	
	Henry daughter of Milly Born Sept 2	1816	
	Mary daughter of Jinny Born Feby	1818	
	Frederick Augustos son of Harriott Feby	1818	
	James Son of Cate Born May 27	1819	died
	Nancy Daughter of Milly Born July —	1819	
	Isaac son of Jinny Born aug 10	1819	
	Henry son of old Betto Born Feby	1820	

165

Record of Douglass's birth in February 1818

12

demonstrated to Douglass the power of both the written word and oratory—a profoundly influential lesson.

In 1833, when Douglass was about fifteen, a quarrel between Hugh Auld and his brother Thomas, who had become Douglass's legal owner, resulted in Douglass's return to the Eastern Shore. Master and slave clashed, and Thomas soon hired Douglass out to a local "slave breaker," Edward Covey, who put Douglass to work as a field hand. Douglass endured repeated whippings and humiliations from Covey, recalling himself as "broken in body, soul, and spirit . . . a man transformed into a brute." But six months into his term with the slave breaker, Douglass fought back. The result was a draw, but Douglass was transformed, his self-confidence restored and his determination to be free renewed.

Douglass made a failed attempt to escape slavery when he was about eighteen, leading Thomas Auld to send him back to Hugh Auld to learn the caulking trade in the Baltimore shipyards. (Caulkers made a boat watertight by packing seams with a material like oakum or pitch.) In 1837, Douglass joined the East Baltimore Mental Improvement Society, a debating group of free black caulkers. He was the only member who was also a slave. By talking to other members, Douglass learned what life as a free black man was like. He also met his future wife, Anna Murray, a free black housekeeper, through the society. In contrast to Douglass, Anna was illiterate; she would remain so all her life, despite attempts by a tutor and her daughter Rosetta to teach her to read.

With Anna's help, Douglass planned his second escape attempt. On September 3, 1838, he disguised himself as a free black sailor and boarded a northbound train out of Baltimore. After passing through Delaware and Philadelphia and taking a total of three trains and four ferries, he arrived in New York on the following day. He wrote for Anna to join him, and the two were married by the Reverend James W. C. Pennington, another escaped Maryland slave, on September 15, 1838.

The couple moved to New Bedford, Massachusetts, a few days later. Frederick, who had been using the surname Johnson since his arrival in New York, took the last name Douglass at the suggestion of a friend, as Johnson was already a very familiar name in town. Douglass got a job as a caulker, but the white workers threatened to quit if he were allowed to practice his trade. Douglass then took unskilled work—sawing wood, shoveling coal, digging cellars, and collecting rubbish—to support himself and his new family. The Douglasses' first child, Rosetta, was born on June 24, 1839. The Douglasses had

Daguerreotype of Douglass made around 1848 that he
reportedly gave to American feminist Susan B. Anthony

four other children: Lewis, Frederick
Jr., Charles Remond, and Annie, born in
1840, 1842, 1844, and 1849, respectively.

Frederick and Anna soon became
well-established and respected members
of New Bedford's black community.
And Douglass was soon drawn to the
abolitionist movement. He began
subscribing to the American abolitionist
William Lloyd Garrison's newspaper
the *Liberator* and attended antislavery
meetings in New Bedford. In 1841,
William C. Coffin, another American
abolitionist, heard Douglass speak in
New Bedford and convinced the young
man to speak about his life as a slave
at a convention on Nantucket held
months later by the Massachusetts
Anti-Slavery Society. It was Douglass's
first great public speech, and the society
was so impressed that it hired Douglass
as a speaker.

For the next few years, Douglass
traveled throughout the North, delivering powerful lectures against slavery
while enduring segregationist attitudes in the so-called free states. He actively
protested against the segregation he faced in trains, churches, and meeting
halls, where he was not treated as the equal of the white antislavery lecturers
with whom he traveled. Douglass encountered trouble of another sort at an
antislavery meeting in Indiana, where he was beaten by a mob. His right hand
was broken in the melee; the fracture was not properly set, and Douglass never
regained full use of that hand.

As Douglass gained confidence and became a more accomplished orator, he
moved away from recounting his past and began to lecture about the goals of
the antislavery movement. Many people who heard his speeches began to question whether this articulate man had ever truly been a slave. To counter the
rumors, and at the urging of the leadership of the Massachusetts Anti-Slavery

Society, Douglass published *Narrative of the Life of Frederick Douglass, an American Slave, Written by Himself* in 1845. The book was critically acclaimed and sold well both in the United States and Europe.

Because his autobiography revealed details that could lead to his capture as a runaway slave, Douglass sailed to England—and safety—immediately after the publication of the *Narrative*. While Douglass toured England, Ireland, and Scotland, addressing antislavery audiences, Ellen and Anna Richardson, two English friends of Douglass, raised the money to purchase his freedom from Hugh Auld, who had bought the rights to him from Thomas. On December 12, 1846, having received $711.66 (sources vary on the amount), Hugh filed manumission papers in Baltimore, making Douglass legally free.

In 1847 after returning to the United States, Douglass founded the *North Star,* a weekly antislavery paper, in Rochester, New York, and moved his family there. The Douglass home in Rochester became a station on the Underground Railroad for escaped slaves making their way to Canada. Douglass attended the first women's rights convention, held July 19–20, 1848, in Seneca Falls, New York, where he was the only man to speak in favor of Elizabeth Cady Stanton's resolution calling for a woman's right to vote. That same year, he placed his daughter Rosetta in an Albany school after she was asked to leave her private school in Rochester because of her race. Douglass began campaigning for the desegregation of Rochester's public schools—a campaign he eventually won in 1857.

Douglass decided in 1851 to merge the *North Star* with the *Liberty Party Paper,* published by Gerrit Smith, a prominent abolitionist and a founder of the Liberty Party. The new publication would be known as *Frederick Douglass' Paper,* which Douglass

Anna Murray Douglass, Douglass's first wife

Helen Pitts Douglass, Douglass's second wife, whom he married in 1884

published until 1860. He continued to publish *Douglass' Monthly,* a supplement to the *Paper,* until 1863.

The formation of the new paper coincided with Douglass's adoption of an antislavery interpretation of the U.S. Constitution—a controversial position and a reversal of his earlier one. His position caused a rift with Garrison and the American Anti-Slavery Society. Now Douglass believed that not only was there a moral argument to be made against slavery, but also a political one. Whatever the intent or beliefs of the framers, the language of the Constitution, he decided, was opposed to the existence of slavery.

Throughout the 1850s, Douglass continued to deliver lectures against slavery, as well as lectures opposing segregation in the North, supporting women's rights, and denouncing capital punishment. In 1855, Douglass published his second autobiography, *My Bondage and My Freedom,* which sold 15,000 copies in two months. In 1856, he met the abolitionist John Brown, who was advocating armed resistance to slavery. Douglass remained a friend and supporter of Brown until 1859, when Brown shared his plan to seize the federal arsenal in Harpers Ferry, Virginia (now West Virginia), and arm slaves in the area. Douglass refused to endorse the plan. When Brown and his supporters were captured after occupying the arsenal, authorities found a letter Douglass had written to Brown and charged him as an accomplice. Warned by a telegraph operator that he would soon be arrested, Douglass fled to Canada and then to England, where he began a previously scheduled speaking tour.

During the U.S. Civil War (1861–1865), Douglass became a recruiter for the famed 54th Massachusetts Volunteers, the first regiment of black soldiers raised by a Northern state. His sons Charles and Lewis eventually joined the regiment, and son Frederick Jr. later became a recruiter. Black soldiers earned less pay, rose more slowly in the ranks, and were frequently murdered if captured by Confederate troops. Douglass met with President Abraham Lincoln in 1863 to urge him to address these issues. Douglass and Lincoln also met numerous times to discuss slavery and the status of blacks once the war was over. In the event of a negotiated peace, Lincoln hoped Douglass would assist in helping slaves escape to the North. Although Douglass was critical of many of the president's policies, he hailed the Emancipation Proclamation and ultimately supported Lincoln's bid for reelection in 1864. After Lincoln was assassinated, Mary Todd Lincoln gave Douglass his walking stick as a memorial gift.

Although Douglass continued his career as a reformer and a champion of human rights after emancipation, he also joined the political establishment, becoming the first black citizen to hold high rank in the federal government. In the years following the Civil War, Douglass put his energy into campaigning for the right of black men to vote, which culminated in the passage of the Fifteenth Amendment in 1870. In 1872, after his Rochester house was destroyed by a fire possibly set by an arsonist, he moved his family to Washington, D.C., where he had been living for two years. The new Equal Rights Party nominated Douglass as their candidate for vice president in the 1872 election, but he declined the nomination. The party's candidate for president was Victoria C. Woodhull, a controversial feminist and suffragist. In 1877, President Rutherford B. Hayes appointed Douglass as U.S. marshal for the District of Columbia. He served as marshal until 1881, when James A. Garfield became president. Garfield made Douglass recorder of deeds for the District of Columbia, a lesser position, which he held until 1886. With more time to write because these positions enabled him to lecture less often, Douglass published the third of his autobiographies, *Life and Times of Frederick Douglass,* in 1881, but it was a commercial failure. For two years, beginning in 1889, Douglass served as U.S. minister and consul general to Haiti, whose struggle for independence later became one of his lecture topics.

Douglass's wife Anna died in 1882. Two years later, he married Helen Pitts, a white woman and feminist activist who worked as a clerk in the recorder's office. Neither of them was prepared for the hostility of some reactions to their marriage, from friends and family members as well as the general public. Douglass's children were not pleased, and Pitts's father, a former abolitionist and acquaintance of Douglass, would not let Douglass enter his house.

On February 20, 1895, Douglass delivered a rousing speech to the National Council of Women in Washington, D.C. He died of heart failure after returning home that day. To the last day of his life, Douglass continued his tireless pursuit of equal rights for all. In his own time, Douglass gained a reputation as the preeminent spokesperson for African Americans. Not until the U.S. civil rights movement of the 1950s and 1960s, and the broader attention it brought to African American writers, did Douglass's *Narrative* take its place as not only an unsurpassed slave narrative, but also a classic example of American autobiography.

Fugitive Slave Law Convention, Cazenovia, New York, 1850

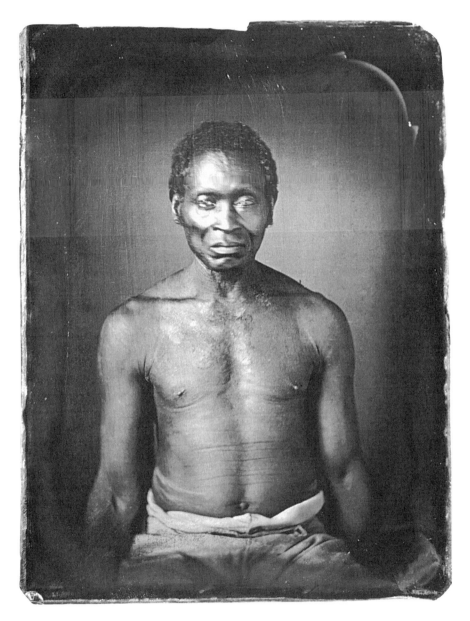

Joseph T. Zealy, "Fassena" (1850). Seeking evidence for his theory of fundamental racial differences, Louis Agassiz, a Harvard University professor, commissioned photographs of American slaves from different regions of Africa and their American-born children. This is one of fifteen surviving daguerreotypes made by Zealy.

Douglass delivered this address in Rochester, New York, on Monday, July 5, 1852.

What to the Slave
Is the Fourth of July?

(SELECTION)

Frederick Douglass

Mr. President, Friends, and Fellow Citizens: He who could address this audience without a quailing sensation has stronger nerves than I have. I do not remember ever to have appeared as a speaker before any assembly more shrinkingly, nor with greater distrust of my ability, than I do this day. A feeling has crept over me, quite unfavorable to the exercise of my limited powers of speech. The task before me is one which requires much previous thought and study for its proper performance. I know that apologies of this sort are generally considered flat and unmeaning. I trust, however, that mine will not be so considered. Should I seem at ease, my appearance would much misrepresent me. The little experience I have had in addressing public meetings, in country school-houses, avails me nothing on the present occasion.

The papers and placards say that I am to deliver a Fourth [of] July oration. This certainly sounds large, and out of the common way, for me. It is true that I have often had the privilege to speak in this beautiful hall, and to address many who now honor me with their presence. But neither their familiar faces, nor the perfect gage I think I have of Corinthian Hall, seems to free me from embarrassment.

The fact is, ladies and gentlemen, the distance between this platform and the slave plantation, from which I escaped, is considerable—and the difficulties to be overcome in getting from the latter to the former are by no means slight. That I am here today is, to me, a matter of astonishment as well as of gratitude. You will not, therefore, be surprised, if in what I have to say, I evince no elaborate preparation, nor grace my speech with any high-sounding exordium. With little experience and with less learning, I have been able to throw my thoughts hastily and imperfectly together; and trusting to your patient and generous indulgence, I will proceed to lay them before you.

This, for the purpose of this celebration, is the Fourth of July. It is the birth-day of your national independence and of your political freedom. This, to you, is what the Passover was to the emancipated people of God. It carries your minds back to the day, and to the act of your great deliverance; and to the signs, and to the wonders, associated with that act and that day. This celebration also marks the beginning of another year of your national life, and reminds you that the Republic of America is now seventy-six years old. I am glad, fellow citizens, that your nation is so young. Seventy-six years, though a good old age for a man, is but a mere speck in the life of a nation. Three score years and ten is the allotted time for individual men, but nations number their years by thousands. According to this fact, you are, even now, only in the beginning of your national career, still lingering in the period of childhood. I repeat, I am glad this is so. There is hope in the thought, and hope is much needed, under the dark clouds which lower above the horizon. The eye of the reformer is met with angry flashes, portending disas-trous times; but his heart may well beat lighter at the thought that America is young, and that she is still in the impressible stage of her existence. May he not hope that high lessons of wisdom, of justice, and of truth, will yet give direction to her destiny? Were the nation older, the patriot's heart might be sadder, and the reformer's brow heavier. Its future might be shrouded in gloom, and the hope of its prophets go out in sorrow. There is consolation in the thought that America is young. Great streams are not easily turned from channels, worn deep in the course of ages. They may sometimes rise in quiet and stately majesty, and inun-date the land, refreshing and fertilizing the earth with their mysterious proper-ties. They may also rise in wrath and fury, and bear away, on their angry waves, the accumulated wealth of years of toil and hardship. They, however, gradually flow back to the same old channel and flow on as serenely as ever. But while the river may not be turned aside, it may dry up, and leave nothing behind but the withered branch and the unsightly rock, to howl in the abyss-sweeping wind, the sad tale of departed glory. As with rivers so with nations.

Fellow citizens, I shall not presume to dwell at length on the associations that cluster about this day. The simple story of it is that, seventy-six years ago, the people of this country were British subjects. The style and title of your "sovereign people" (in which you now glory) was not then born. You were under the British Crown. Your fathers esteemed the English government as the home government, and England as the fatherland. This home government, you know, although a considerable distance from your home, did, in the exercise of its parental prerogatives, impose upon its colonial children such restraints, burdens, and limitations as, in its mature judgment, it deemed wise, right, and proper.

But your fathers, who had not adopted the fashionable idea of this day, of the infallibility of government and the absolute character of its acts, presumed to differ from the home government in respect to the wisdom and the justice of some of those burdens and restraints. They went so far in their excitement as to pronounce the measures of government unjust, unreasonable, and oppressive, and altogether such as ought not to be quietly submitted to. I scarcely need say, fellow citizens, that my opinion of those measures fully accords with that of your fathers. Such a declaration of agreement on my part would not be worth much to anybody. It would, certainly, prove nothing as to what part I might have taken had I lived during the great controversy of 1776. To say *now* that America was right, and England wrong, is exceedingly easy. Everybody can say it; the dastard, not less than the noble brave, can flippantly discant on the tyranny of England toward the American colonies. It is fashionable to do so; but there was a time when to pronounce against England, and in favor of the cause of the colonies, tried men's souls. They who did so were accounted in their day plotters of mischief, agitators and rebels, dangerous men. To side with the right, against the wrong, with the weak against the strong, and with the oppressed against the oppressor! *here* lies the merit, and the one which, of all others, seems unfashionable in our day. The cause of liberty may be stabbed by the men who glory in the deeds of your fathers. But, to proceed.

Feeling themselves harshly and unjustly treated by the home government, your fathers, like men of honesty and men of spirit, earnestly sought redress. They petitioned and remonstrated; they did so in a decorous, respectful, and loyal manner. Their conduct was wholly unexceptionable. This, however, did not answer the purpose. They saw themselves treated with sovereign indifference, coldness, and scorn. Yet they persevered. They were not the men to look back.

As the sheet anchor takes a firmer hold when the ship is tossed by the storm, so did the cause of your fathers grow stronger as it breasted the chilling blasts of kingly displeasure. The greatest and best of British statesmen admitted its justice, and the loftiest eloquence of the British Senate came to its support. But, with that blindness which seems to be the unvarying characteristic of tyrants since Pharoah and his hosts were drowned in the Red Sea, the British government persisted in the exactions complained of.

The madness of this course, we believe, is admitted now, even by England; but we fear the lesson is wholly lost on our present rulers.

Oppression makes a wise man mad. Your fathers were wise men, and if they did not go mad, they became restive under this treatment. They felt themselves the victims of grievous wrongs, wholly incurable in their colonial capacity. With brave men there is always a remedy for oppression. Just here, the idea of a total separation of the colonies from the crown was born! It was a startling idea, much more so than we, at this distance of time, regard it. The timid and the prudent (as has been intimated) of that day, were, of course, shocked and alarmed by it.

Such people lived then, had lived before, and will probably ever have a place on this planet; and their course, in respect to any great change (no matter how great the good to be attained or the wrong to be redressed by it), may be calculated with as much precision as can be the course of the stars. They hate all changes but silver, gold, and copper change! Of this sort of change they are always strongly in favor.

These people were called Tories in the days of your fathers; and the appellation probably conveyed the same idea that is meant by a more modern, though a somewhat less euphonious term, which we often find in our papers, applied to some of our old politicians.

Their opposition to the then dangerous thought was earnest and powerful; but, amid all their terror and affrighted vociferations against it, the alarming and revolutionary idea moved on, and the country with it.

On the second of July, 1776, the old Continental Congress, to the dismay of the lovers of ease and the worshippers of property, clothed that dreadful idea with all the authority of national sanction. They did so in the form of a resolution; and as we seldom hit upon resolutions drawn up in our day whose transparency is at all equal to this, it may refresh your minds and help my story if I read it:

> Resolved, That these united colonies *are,* and of right, ought to be free and Independent States; that they are absolved from all allegiance to the British Crown; and that all political connection between them and the State of Great Britain *is,* and ought to be, dissolved.

Citizens, your fathers made good that resolution. They succeeded, and today you reap the fruits of their success. The freedom gained is yours; and you, therefore, may properly celebrate this anniversary. The Fourth of July is the first great fact in your nation's history—the very ringbolt in the chain of your yet undeveloped destiny.

Pride and patriotism, not less than gratitude, prompt you to celebrate and to hold it in perpetual remembrance. I have said that the Declaration of Independence is the RINGBOLT to the chain of your nation's destiny; so, indeed, I regard it. The principles contained in that instrument are saving principles. Stand by those principles, be true to them on all occasions, in all places, against all foes, and at whatever cost.

From the round top of your ship of state, dark and threatening clouds may be seen. Heavy billows, like mountains in the distance, disclose to the leeward huge forms of flinty rocks! That *bolt* drawn, that *chain* broken, and all is lost. *Cling to this day—cling to it*, and to its principles, with the grasp of a storm-tossed mariner to a spar at midnight.

The coming into being of a nation, in any circumstances, is an interesting event. But, besides general considerations, there were peculiar circumstances which make the advent of this republic an event of special attractiveness.

Undated engraving showing Douglass addressing a British audience during his visit to London in 1846

The whole scene, as I look back to it, was simple, dignified, and sublime.

The population of the country, at the time, stood at the insignificant number of three million. The country was poor in the munitions of war. The population was weak and scattered, and the country a wilderness unsubdued. There were then no means of concert and combination such as exist now. Neither steam nor lightning had then been reduced to order and discipline. From the Potomac to the Delaware was a journey of many days. Under these and innumerable other disadvantages, your fathers declared for liberty and independence and triumphed.

Fellow citizens, I am not wanting in respect for the fathers of this republic. The signers of the Declaration of Independence were brave men. They were great men, too—great enough to give fame to a great age. It does not often happen to a nation to raise, at one time, such a number of truly great men. The point from which I am compelled to view them is not, certainly, the most favorable; and yet I cannot contemplate their great deeds with less than admiration. They were statesmen, patriots, and heroes, and for the good they did and the principles they contended for, I will unite with you to honor their memory.

They loved their country better than their own private interests; and, though this is not the highest form of human excellence, all will concede that it is a rare virtue, and that when it is exhibited, it ought to command respect. He who will, intelligently, lay down his life for his country is a man whom it is not in human nature to despise. Your fathers staked their lives, their fortunes, and their sacred honor on the cause of their country. In their admiration of liberty, they lost sight of all other interests.

They were peace men, but they preferred revolution to peaceful submission to bondage. They were quiet men, but they did not shrink from agitating against oppression. They showed forbearance, but that they knew its limits. They believed in order, but not in the order of tyranny. With them, nothing was "settled" that was not right. With them, justice, liberty, and humanity were "final," not slavery and oppression. You may well cherish the memory of such men. They were great in their day and generation. Their solid manhood stands out the more as we contrast it with these degenerate times.

How circumspect, exact, and proportionate were all their movements! How unlike the politicians of an hour! Their statesmanship looked beyond the passing moment and stretched away in strength into the distant future. They seized upon eternal principles and set a glorious example in their defense. Mark them!

Fully appreciating the hardship to be encountered, firmly believing in the right of their cause, honorably inviting the scrutiny of an onlooking world, reverently appealing to heaven to attest their sincerity, soundly comprehending the solemn responsibility they were about to assume, wisely measuring the terrible odds against them, your fathers, the fathers of this republic, did, most deliberately, under the inspiration of a glorious patriotism, and with a sublime faith in the great principles of justice and freedom, lay deep the cornerstone of the national super-structure, which has risen and still rises in grandeur around you.

Of this fundamental work, this day is the anniversary. Our eyes are met with demonstrations of joyous enthusiasm. Banners and pennants wave exultingly on the breeze. The din of business, too, is hushed. Even Mammon seems to have quitted his grasp on this day. The ear-piercing fife and the stirring drum unite their accents with the ascending peal of a thousand church bells. Prayers are made, hymns are sung, and sermons are preached in honor of this day; while the quick martial tramp of a great and multitudinous nation, echoed back by all the hills, valleys, and mountains of a vast continent, bespeak the occasion one of thrilling and universal interest—a nation's jubilee.

Friends and citizens, I need not enter further into the causes which led to this anniversary. Many of you understand them better than I do. You could instruct me in regard to them. That is a branch of knowledge in which you feel, perhaps, a much deeper interest than your speaker. The causes which led to the separation of the colonies from the British Crown have never lacked for a tongue. They have all been taught in your common schools, narrated at your firesides, unfolded from your pulpits, and thundered from your legislative halls, and are as familiar to you as household words. They form the staple of your national poetry and eloquence.

I remember, also, that, as a people, Americans are remarkably familiar with all facts which make in their own favor. This is esteemed by some as a national trait—perhaps a national weakness. It is a fact that whatever makes for the wealth or for the reputation of Americans, and can be had *cheap!* will be found by Americans. I shall not be charged with slandering Americans if I say I think the American side of any question may be safely left in American hands.

I leave, therefore, the great deeds of your fathers to other gentlemen whose claim to have been regularly descended will be less likely to be disputed than mine!

My business, if I have any here today, is with the present. The accepted time with God and his cause is the ever-living now:

> Trust no future, however pleasant,
>   Let the dead past bury its dead;
> Act, act in the living present,
>   Heart within, and God overhead.[1]

We have to do with the past only as we can make it useful to the present and to the future. To all inspiring motives, to noble deeds which can be gained from the past,

1. [Stanza quoted from Henry Wadsworth Longfellow's poem "A Psalm of Life."—EDS.]

27

we are welcome. But now is the time, the important time. Your fathers have lived, died, and have done their work, and have done much of it well. You live and must die, and you must do your work. You have no right to enjoy a child's share in the labor of your fathers unless your children are to be blest by your labors. You have no right to wear out and waste the hard-earned fame of your fathers to cover your indolence. Sydney Smith tells us that men seldom eulogize the wisdom and virtues of their fathers but to excuse some folly or wickedness of their own. This truth is not a doubtful one. There are illustrations of it near and remote, ancient and modern. It was fashionable, hundreds of years ago, for the children of Jacob to boast, we have "Abraham to our father," when they had long lost Abraham's faith and spirit. That people contented themselves under the shadow of Abraham's great name, while they repudiated the deeds which made his name great. Need I remind you that a similar thing is being done all over this country today? Need I tell you that the Jews are not the only people who built the tombs of the prophets and garnished the sepulchers of the righteous? Washington could not die till he had broken the chains of his slaves. Yet his monument is built up by the price of human blood, and the traders in the bodies and souls of men shout, "We have Washington to *our father*." Alas! that it should be so, yet so it is:

> The evil that men do, lives after them,
> The good is oft' interred with their bones.[2]

Fellow citizens, pardon me, allow me to ask, why am I called upon to speak here today? What have I, or those I represent, to do with your national independence? Are the great principles of political freedom and of natural justice, embodied in that Declaration of Independence, extended to us? And am I, therefore, called upon to bring our humble offering to the national altar, and to confess the benefits and express devout gratitude for the blessings resulting from your independence to us?

Would to God, both for your sakes and ours, that an affirmative answer could be truthfully returned to these questions! Then would my task be light, and my burden easy and delightful. For *who* is there so cold, that a nation's sympathy could not warm him? Who so obdurate and dead to the claims of gratitude, that would not thankfully acknowledge such priceless benefits? Who so stolid and selfish, that would not give his voice to swell the hallelujahs of a nation's jubilee, when the

---

2. [Shakespeare, *Julius Caesar* 3.2 76–77.—EDS.]

chains of servitude had been torn from his limbs? I am not that man. In a case like that, the dumb might eloquently speak, and the "lame man leap as an hart."

But such is not the state of the case. I say it with a sad sense of the disparity between us. I am not included within the pale of this glorious anniversary! Your high independence only reveals the immeasurable distance between us. The blessings in which you, this day, rejoice, are not enjoyed in common. The rich inheritance of justice, liberty, prosperity, and independence, bequeathed by your fathers, is shared by you, not by me. The sunlight that brought life and healing to you has brought stripes and death to me. This Fourth [of] July is *yours*, not *mine. You* may rejoice, *I* must mourn. To drag a man in fetters into the grand illuminated temple of liberty, and call upon him to join you in joyous anthems, were inhuman mockery and sacrilegious irony. Do you mean, citizens, to mock me, by asking me to speak today? If so, there is a parallel to your conduct. And let me warn you that it is dangerous to copy the example of a nation whose crimes, towering up to heaven, were thrown down by the breath of the Almighty, burying that nation in irrecoverable ruin! I can today take up the plaintive lament of a peeled and woe-smitten people!

"By the rivers of Babylon, there we sat down. Yea! we wept when we remembered Zion. We hanged our harps upon the willows in the midst thereof. For there, they that carried us away captive, required of us a song; and they who wasted us required of us mirth, saying, Sing us one of the songs of Zion. How can we sing the Lord's song in a strange land? If I forget thee, O Jerusalem, let my right hand forget her cunning. If I do not remember thee, let my tongue cleave to the roof of my mouth."[3]

Fellow citizens, above your national, tumultuous joy, I hear the mournful wail of millions! whose chains, heavy and grievous yesterday, are today rendered more intolerable by the jubilee shouts that reach them. If I do forget, if I do not faithfully remember those bleeding children of sorrow this day, "may my right hand forget her cunning, and may my tongue cleave to the roof of my mouth!" To forget them, to pass lightly over their wrongs, and to chime in with the popular theme would be treason most scandalous and shocking, and would make me a reproach before God and the world. My subject, then, fellow citizens, is AMERICAN SLAVERY. I shall see this day, and its popular characteristics, from the slave's point of view. Standing there, identified with the American bondman, making his

---

3. [This and the first quotation in the paragraph below are from Psalms 137.1–6.—EDS.]

wrongs mine, I do not hesitate to declare, with all my soul, that the character and conduct of this nation never looked blacker to me than on this Fourth of July! Whether we turn to the declarations of the past or to the professions of the present, the conduct of the nation seems equally hideous and revolting. America is false to the past, false to the present, and solemnly binds herself to be false to the future. Standing with God and the crushed and bleeding slave on this occasion, I will, in the name of humanity which is outraged, in the name of liberty which is fettered, in the name of the Constitution and the Bible, which are disregarded and trampled upon, dare to call in question and to denounce, with all the emphasis I can command, everything that serves to perpetuate slavery—the great sin and shame of America! "I will not equivocate; I will not excuse;"[4] I will use the severest language I can command; and yet not one word shall escape me that any man, whose judgment is not blinded by prejudice, or who is not at heart a slaveholder, shall not confess to be right and just.

But I fancy I hear some one of my audience say, it is just in this circumstance that you and your brother abolitionists fail to make a favorable impression on the public mind. Would you argue more, and denounce less, would you persuade more, and rebuke less, your cause would be much more likely to succeed. But, I submit, where all is plain there is nothing to be argued. What point in the anti-slavery creed would you have me argue? On what branch of the subject do the people of this country need light? Must I undertake to prove that the slave is a man? That point is conceded already. Nobody doubts it. The slaveholders themselves acknowledge it in the enactment of laws for their government. They acknowledge it when they punish disobedience on the part of the slave. There are seventy-two crimes in the State of Virginia which, if committed by a black man (no matter how ignorant he be), subject him to the punishment of death, while only two of the same crimes will subject a white man to the like punishment. What is this but the acknowledgment that the slave is a moral, intellectual, and responsible being? The manhood of the slave is conceded. It is admitted in the fact that Southern statute books are covered with enactments forbidding, under severe fines and penalties, the teaching of the slave to read or to write. When you can point to any such laws in reference to the beasts of the field, then I may consent to argue the manhood of the slave. When the dogs in your streets, when the fowls of the air,

4. [From the first issue of the *Liberator* (January 1, 1831), in which William Lloyd
   Garrison promised, "I am in earnest—I will not equivocate—I will not excuse—I
   will not retreat a single inch—and I will be heard."—EDS.]

when the cattle on your hills, when the fish of the sea, and the reptiles that crawl shall be unable to distinguish the slave from a brute, *then* will I argue with you that the slave is a man!

For the present, it is enough to affirm the equal manhood of the Negro race. It is not astonishing that, while we are ploughing, planting, and reaping, using all kinds of mechanical tools, erecting houses, constructing bridges, building ships, working in metals of brass, iron, copper, silver, and gold; that, while we are reading, writing, and cyphering, acting as clerks, merchants, and secretaries, having among us lawyers, doctors, ministers, poets, authors, editors, orators, and teachers; that, while we are engaged in all manner of enterprises common to other men, digging gold in California, capturing the whale in the Pacific, feeding sheep and cattle on the hillside, living, moving, acting, thinking, planning, living in families as husbands, wives, and children, and, above all, confessing and worshipping the Christian's God, and looking hopefully for life and immortality beyond the grave, we are called upon to prove that we are men!

Would you have me argue that man is entitled to liberty? That he is the rightful owner of his own body? You have already declared it. Must I argue the wrongfulness of slavery? Is that a question for Republicans? Is it to be settled by the rules of logic and argumentation, as a matter beset with great difficulty, involving a doubtful application of the principle of justice, hard to be understood? How should I look today, in the presence of Americans, dividing and subdividing a discourse to show that men have a natural right to freedom? speaking of it relatively, and positively, negatively, and affirmatively. To do so would be to make myself ridiculous, and to offer an insult to your understanding. There is not a man beneath the canopy of heaven that does not know that slavery is wrong *for him*.

What, am I to argue that it is wrong to make men brutes, to rob them of their liberty, to work them without wages, to keep them ignorant of their relations to their fellow men, to beat them with sticks, to flay their flesh with the lash, to load their limbs with irons, to hunt them with dogs, to sell them at auction, to sunder their families, to knock out their teeth, to burn their flesh, to starve them into obedience and submission to their masters? Must I argue that a system thus marked with blood and stained with pollution is *wrong*? No! I will not. I have better employments for my time and strength than such arguments would imply.

What, then, remains to be argued? Is it that slavery is not divine; that God did not establish it; that our doctors of divinity are mistaken? There is blasphemy in the thought. That which is inhuman cannot be divine! *Who* can reason on such a proposition? They that can, may; I cannot. The time for such argument is past.

At a time like this, scorching irony, not convincing argument, is needed. O! had I the ability, and could I reach the nation's ear, I would, today, pour out a fiery stream of biting ridicule, blasting reproach, withering sarcasm, and stern rebuke. For it is not light that is needed, but fire; it is not the gentle shower, but thunder. We need the storm, the whirlwind, and the earthquake. The feeling of the nation must be quickened; the conscience of the nation must be roused; the propriety of the nation must be startled, the hypocrisy of the nation must be exposed; and its crimes against God and man must be proclaimed and denounced.

What, to the American slave, is your Fourth of July? I answer: a day that reveals to him, more than all other days in the year, the gross injustice and cruelty to which he is the constant victim. To him, your celebration is a sham; your boasted liberty, an unholy license; your national greatness, swelling vanity; your sounds of rejoicing are empty and heartless; your denunciations of tyrants, brass-fronted impudence; your shouts of liberty and equality, hollow mockery; your prayers and hymns, your sermons and thanksgivings, with all your religious parade and solemnity, are, to him, mere bombast, fraud, deception, impiety, and hypocrisy—a thin veil to cover up crimes which would disgrace a nation of savages. There is not a nation on the earth guilty of practices more shocking and bloody than are the people of these United States, at this very hour.

Go where you may, search where you will, roam through all the monarchies and despotisms of the Old World, travel through South America, search out every abuse, and when you have found the last, lay your facts by the side of the everyday practices of this nation, and you will say with me that, for revolting barbarity and shameless hypocrisy, America reigns without a rival.

Gordon, a Mississippi slave,
photographed around 1863 after
he escaped to Union forces

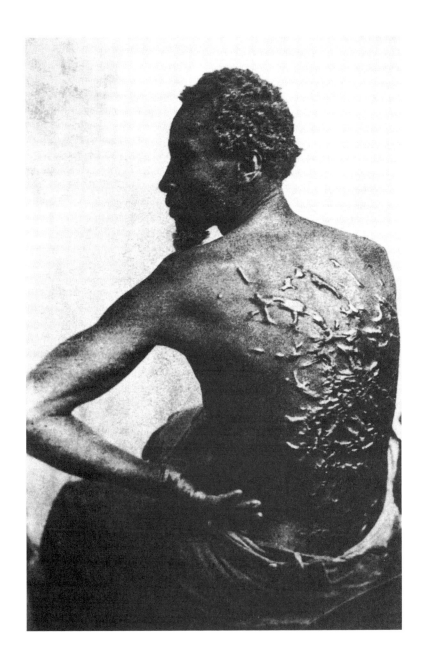

Interpretive Questions for Discussion

1. Why does Douglass begin his speech with a lengthy apology for his lack of ability and preparedness?

2. Why does Douglass compare the Fourth of July to Passover?

3. When Douglass refers to the American people and their history, why does he use "you" and "your" instead of "we" and "our"? Doesn't he consider himself American? (22–23)

4. Why does Douglass point out that the signers of the Declaration of Independence "were accounted in their day plotters of mischief, agitators and rebels, dangerous men"? (23)

5. What does Douglass mean when he says that "oppression makes a wise man mad"? (24)

6. Douglass says that the signers of the Declaration of Independence "loved their country better than their own private interests." Why does he add that "this is not the highest form of human excellence"? (26)

7. Why does Douglass say that the familiarity of Americans "with all facts which make in their own favor" is "perhaps a national weakness"? (27)

8. Why does Douglass praise the nation's founders during the first part of his speech? How does he believe the story of the American Revolution can be "useful" to the present and to the future? (27)

9. How does Douglass counter those who say that he should "argue more, and denounce less"? (30)

10. Does Douglass employ a tone of "scorching irony" in this speech? (32)

NARRATIVE OF THE
LIFE OF FREDERICK DOUGLASS

Interpretive Questions
for Discussion

The following questions suggest a wide range of possibilities for interpretation.
Some of the questions are keyed to the passages for close reading
(pp. 47–63), and careful reading of these passages either before or during
the discussion allows you to consider the various possible answers
to the discussion questions more thoroughly.

Keep in mind that everyone, including the discussion leader, is an
equal partner in interpretation and understanding. Do not expect a teacher
or leader to provide answers to the questions that follow;
instead, listen to individual ideas during discussion, test the validity
of your own thoughts, and learn from the group.

Questions have been organized for discussion of the book as a whole or by chapter.

What enables Douglass to survive and eventually escape his life as a slave?

1. How is Douglass able to think of himself as fully human despite the dehumanizing effects of slavery?

2. How does Douglass develop a moral sense different from the kind that most slaves possess as a result of the conditions in which they are forced to live?

Passage 2

3. What role does learning to read ultimately play in the development of Douglass's personality and his escape from slavery? Why does he describe his owner's refusal to allow him to learn to read as "shutting me up in mental darkness"?

4. As he begins to describe his last six months with Mr. Covey, why does Douglass say that "you shall see how a slave was made a man"?

5. How does Douglass maintain his religious faith when his owners use theirs to justify their treatment of him? How does Douglass differentiate his faith from theirs?

6. To what extent does Douglass see himself as exceptional, and to what extent as representative of all slaves?

According to Douglass, how does slavery degrade both slaves and masters?

1. Why does Douglass point out the harm done to whites by slavery?

2. When Douglass writes, "You have seen how a man was made a slave; you shall see how a slave was made a man," what does he understand a man to be?

3. According to Douglass, why is hypocrisy essential to the smooth operation of slavery? Why does he believe it is destructive to both the slave and the master?

4. When Douglass says that his battle with Mr. Covey marked "the turning-point in my career as a slave," is he suggesting that violent resistance is necessary to oppose violent oppression? *Passage 6*

5. What is Douglass's attitude toward the suffering he experienced as a slave? How does his attitude affect your response to the actions and incidents he portrays?

Preface

1. When Garrison writes that Douglass needed "a comparatively small amount of cultivation to make him an ornament to society and a blessing to his race," is he implying that Douglass is exceptional or that all slaves are capable of such "high attainments"?

2. Why does Garrison make a point of emphasizing that Douglass's *Narrative* is "entirely his own production"?

3. When Garrison asks his readers whether they are on the side of "the man-stealers" or "their down-trodden victims," is he appealing to their sense of shame or to their sense of justice?

Chapter 1

1. Why does Douglass begin his narrative by focusing on the fact that most slaves do not know their birthdays?

2. Why does the whipping of his Aunt Hester affect Douglass so deeply? What insights does it give him about the nature and psychology of slavery?

Chapter 2

1. What does it say about the effect of slavery on the moral development of its victims that slaves could regard as "good" an overseer who "whipped, but seemed to take no pleasure in it"?

2. What does Douglass mean when he says that "the same traits of character might be seen in Colonel Lloyd's slaves, as are seen in the slaves of the political parties"?

Passage 1 3. Why does Douglass believe that hearing the slaves "sing most exultingly" of going to the Great House Farm "would do more to impress some minds with the horrible character of slavery, than the reading of whole volumes of philosophy on the subject could do"?

4. Why does Douglass describe slaves who go to the Great House Farm as "peculiarly enthusiastic"?

Chapter 3

1. Why does Colonel Lloyd go to extreme lengths to protect his "finely culti-vated garden" from the "hungry swarms of boys" intent on stealing its fruit? What does Douglass mean when he says that few slaves had "the virtue or the vice to resist it"?

2. Why does Douglass say that the willingness of slaves to "suppress the truth rather than take the consequences of telling it" proves that they are "a part of the human family"?

3. When Douglass notes that slaves "seemed to think that the greatness of their masters was transferable to themselves," does he consider this tendency a normal part of human psychology or a peculiar effect of slavery?

Chapter 4

1. Why does Mr. Gore do "nothing reluctantly, no matter how disagreeable"?

2. Does Douglass believe Gore's murder of Demby is motivated more by evil intent or by a genuine belief in the necessity of his action?

3. Why does Douglass note that Gore's "horrid crime was not even submitted to judicial investigation"?

4. After making the point that, in Maryland, slaves are murdered with impunity, why does Douglass then present additional examples?

Chapter 5

1. Why does the prospect of moving to Baltimore, where he will remain a slave, inspire Douglass with "the highest hopes of future happiness"?

2. In saying that going to Baltimore was "the first plain manifestation of that kind providence which has ever since attended me," is Douglass saying that his own actions and character traits were not primarily responsible for his fate?

3. Why does Douglass say that his belief in "a special interposition of divine Providence" may be "deemed superstitious, and even egotistical"?

Chapter 6

Passage 2   1. Is learning to read what makes Douglass "forever unfit" to be a slave?

Passage 2   2. Why does Mr. Auld claim that learning will make Douglass "discontented and unhappy"? When is Douglass more discontented and unhappy, before or after he starts to educate himself? Why?

Passage 2   3. Once the young Douglass understands "the white man's power to enslave the black man," why does he consider it "a grand achievement"?

Chapter 7

1. Douglass says that his mistress needed "some training in the exercise of irresponsible power." Does he believe that some people inherently possess qualities that enable them to hold slaves, while others do not?

2. In describing his mistress's transformation, is Douglass implying that no one put in her position, however morally superior, would be immune to the corrupting power of slavery?

3. When Douglass says of his mistress that slavery proved "as injurious to her as it did to me," is he reducing her responsibility for the way she begins to treat him?

4. Why does Douglass "at times feel that learning to read had been a curse rather than a blessing"? *Passage 3*

5. Upon learning to read, why does Douglass feel that "freedom now appeared, to disappear no more forever"? *Passage 3*

Chapter 8

1. When his old master dies, and Douglass is "sent for, to be valued with the other property," why does this produce in him a "new conception" of his "degraded condition"? Why does the valuation enable Douglass to see "more clearly than ever the brutalizing effects of slavery upon both slave and slaveholder"?

2. Before the valuation, why had Douglass become "insensible" to his lot, or "at least partly so"?

3. In describing his grandmother's situation at the end of her life, why does Douglass quote the poem by John Greenleaf Whittier? *Passage 4*

Chapter 9

1. According to Douglass, why are masters who are not born slaveholders "the worst"?

2. Do Douglass and his fellow slaves feel contempt for Captain (Thomas) Auld primarily because he is so mean, or because he "commanded without firmness"?

3. After describing Thomas Auld's particularly excessive cruelty toward Henny, why does Douglass then say that "Master Thomas was one of the many pious slaveholders who hold slaves for the very charitable purpose of taking care of them"?

Chapter 10

1. Is Douglass being sincere or ironic when he expresses sympathy for Mr. Covey because "he sometimes deceived himself into the solemn belief, that he was a sincere worshiper of the most high God"?

2. Why does Douglass seek the help of Master Thomas after he is severely wounded by Mr. Covey?

3. Why would Douglass believe that the root given to him by Sandy Jenkins may have played a part in his never being whipped again?

4. Why does Douglass describe at length the treatment of slaves under the Reverends Daniel Weeden and Rigby Hopkins?

5. For Douglass, why was teaching other slaves to read the "sweetest engagement with which [he] was ever blessed"?

6. Why does Douglass try to include other slaves in his first plan for escape, even though it requires him to "imbue their minds with thoughts of freedom"?

7. When the first escape attempt fails and Douglass and his fellow slaves are in jail, why do they fear separation "more than any thing this side of death"?

8. Why does any improvement in Douglass's everyday life increase his "desire to be free"?

Chapter 11

1. Why does Douglass make a distinction between the "underground railroad" and what he sees as the "upperground railroad"?

2. Why does Douglass include an "exact copy" of his marriage certificate?

3. Why does Douglass relate the history of his name?

4. Why does Douglass let someone else choose a new last name for him?

5. Why were the circumstances of life in the North unimaginable to Douglass before his arrival in New York?

6. When first asked to speak at an antislavery meeting, why does Douglass say, "I felt myself a slave, and the idea of speaking to white people weighed me down"? Why does Douglass feel "a degree of freedom" after speaking for a few moments?

Appendix

1. According to Douglass, why does acceptance of the "Christianity of Christ" mean rejection of the "Christianity of this land"?

2. Why does Douglass choose to end the appendix with a parody?

HARPER'S WEEKLY.

JOURNAL OF CIVILIZATION.

Vol. XXVII.—No. 1405.
Copyright, 1883, by Harper & Brothers.

NEW YORK, SATURDAY, NOVEMBER 24, 1883.

TEN CENTS A COPY.
WITH A SUPPLEMENT.

FREDERICK DOUGLASS.—[See Page 743.]

NARRATIVE OF THE
LIFE OF FREDERICK DOUGLASS

Passages and Questions
for Close Reading

The questions that follow these passages encourage close reading and, taken together, constitute a rigorous study of literary themes, techniques, and terms. All readers will benefit from the challenges these questions pose, and students in honors courses or courses qualifying for college credit will find these questions useful for exam preparation.

Passage 1

The slaves selected to go to the Great House Farm, for the monthly allowance for themselves and their fellow-slaves, were peculiarly enthusiastic. While on their way, they would make the dense old woods, for miles around, reverberate with their wild songs, revealing at once the highest joy and the deepest sadness. They would compose and sing as they went along, consulting neither time nor tune. The thought that came up, came out—if not in the word, in the sound;— and as frequently in the one as in the other. They would sometimes sing the most pathetic sentiment in the most rapturous tone, and the most rapturous sentiment in the most pathetic tone. Into all of their songs they would manage to weave something of the Great House Farm. Especially would they do this, when leaving home. They would then sing most exultingly the following words:—

> "I am going away to the Great House Farm!
> O, yea! O, yea! O!"

This they would sing, as a chorus, to words which to many would seem unmeaning jargon, but which, nevertheless, were full of meaning to them- selves. I have sometimes thought that the mere hearing of those songs would do more to impress some minds with the horrible character of slavery, than the reading of whole volumes of philosophy on the subject could do.

I did not, when a slave, understand the deep meaning of those rude and apparently incoherent songs. I was myself within the circle; so that I neither saw nor heard as those without might see and hear. They told a tale of woe which was then altogether beyond my feeble comprehension; they were tones loud, long, and deep; they breathed the prayer and complaint of souls boiling over with the bitterest anguish. Every tone was a testimony against slavery, and a prayer to God for deliverance from chains. The hearing of those wild notes always depressed my spirit, and filled me with ineffable sadness. I have frequently found myself in tears while hearing them. The mere recurrence to those songs, even now, afflicts me; and while I am writing these lines, an expres- sion of feeling has already found its way down my cheek. To those songs I trace my first glimmering conception of the dehumanizing character of slavery. I can never get rid of that conception. Those songs still follow me, to deepen my hatred of slavery, and quicken my sympathies for my brethren in bonds. If any one wishes to be impressed with the soul-killing effects of slavery, let him go to Colonel Lloyd's plantation, and, on allowance-day, place himself in the deep pine woods, and there let him, in silence, analyze the sounds that shall pass through the chambers of his soul,—and if he is not thus impressed, it will only be because "there is no flesh in his obdurate heart."

I have often been utterly astonished, since I came to the north, to find persons who could speak of the singing, among slaves, as evidence of their contentment and happiness. It is impossible to conceive of a greater mistake. Slaves sing most when they are most unhappy. The songs of the slave represent the sorrows of his heart; and he is relieved by them, only as an aching heart is relieved by its tears. At least, such is my experience. I have often sung to drown my sorrow, but seldom to express my happiness. Crying for joy, and singing for joy, were alike uncommon to me while in the jaws of slavery. The singing of a man cast away upon a desolate island might be as appropriately considered as evidence of contentment and happiness, as the singing of a slave; the songs of the one and of the other are prompted by the same emotion.

1.   Why is Douglass convinced that hearing the songs sung by slaves reveals "the soul-killing effects of slavery," even though the songs contain expressions of "the highest joy" as well as "the deepest sadness"?

2.   When Douglass quotes the song about the Great House Farm, why does he choose lyrics that, in their literal meaning, seem so innocuous?

3.   Why is Douglass able to understand "the deep meaning of those rude and apparently incoherent songs" only after he is no longer a slave himself?

4.   What is the effect of Douglass telling the reader that, "while I am writing these lines, an expression of feeling has already found its way down my cheek"?

5.   Why do these songs, and not the events he recounts, give Douglass his "first glimmering conception of the dehumanizing character of slavery"?

Passage 2

Very soon after I went to live with Mr. and Mrs. Auld, she very kindly commenced to teach me the A, B, C. After I had learned this, she assisted me in learning to spell words of three or four letters. Just at this point of my progress, Mr. Auld found out what was going on, and at once forbade Mrs. Auld to instruct me further, telling her, among other things, that it was unlawful, as well as unsafe, to teach a slave to read. To use his own words, further, he said, "If you give a nigger an inch, he will take an ell. A nigger should know nothing but to obey his master—to do as he is told to do. Learning would *spoil* the best nigger in the world. Now," said he, "if you teach that nigger (speaking of myself) how to read, there would be no keeping him. It would forever unfit him to be a slave. He would at once become unmanageable, and of no value to his master. As to himself, it could do him no good, but a great deal of harm. It would make him discontented and unhappy." These words sank deep into my heart, stirred up sentiments within that lay slumbering, and called into existence an entirely new train of thought. It was a new and special revelation, explaining dark and mysterious things, with which my youthful understanding had struggled, but struggled in vain. I now understood what had been to me a most perplexing difficulty—to wit, the white man's power to enslave the black man. It was a grand achievement, and I prized it highly. From that moment, I understood the pathway from slavery to freedom. It was just what I wanted, and I got it at a time when I the least expected it. Whilst I was saddened by the thought of losing the aid of my kind mistress, I was gladdened by the invaluable instruction which, by the merest accident, I had gained from my master. Though conscious of the difficulty of learning without a teacher, I set out with high hope, and a fixed purpose, at whatever cost of trouble, to learn how to read. The very decided manner with which he spoke, and strove to impress his wife with the evil consequences of giving me instruction, served to convince me that he was deeply sensible of the truths he was uttering. It gave me the best assurance that I might rely with the utmost confidence on the results which, he said, would flow from teaching me to read. What he most dreaded, that I most desired. What he most loved, that I most hated. That which to him was a great evil, to be carefully shunned, was to me a great good, to be diligently sought;

and the argument which he so warmly urged, against my learning to read, only served to inspire me with a desire and determination to learn. In learning to read, I owe almost as much to the bitter opposition of my master, as to the kindly aid of my mistress. I acknowledge the benefit of both.

1. Why do Mr. Auld's statements enable Douglass to understand "the pathway from slavery to freedom"?

2. What is the effect of the repeated contrasts Douglass draws between himself and his master in each sentence near the end of the passage, beginning with "What he most dreaded, that I most desired"?

3. What is Douglass's tone when he says, with regard to the roles his master and mistress played in his learning to read, "I acknowledge the benefit of both"?

Passage 3

In the same book, I met with one of Sheridan's mighty speeches on and in behalf of Catholic emancipation. These were choice documents to me. I read them over and over again with unabated interest. They gave tongue to interesting thoughts of my own soul, which had frequently flashed through my mind, and died away for want of utterance. The moral which I gained from the dialogue was the power of truth over the conscience of even a slaveholder. What I got from Sheridan was a bold denunciation of slavery, and a powerful vindication of human rights. The reading of these documents enabled me to utter my thoughts, and to meet the arguments brought forward to sustain slavery; but while they relieved me of one difficulty, they brought on another even more painful than the one of which I was relieved. The more I read, the more I was led to abhor and detest my enslavers. I could regard them in no other light than a band of successful robbers, who had left their homes, and gone to Africa, and stolen us from our homes, and in a strange land reduced us to slavery. I loathed them as being the meanest as well as the most wicked of men. As I read and contemplated the subject, behold! that very discontentment which Master Hugh had predicted would follow my learning to read had already come, to torment and sting my soul to unutterable anguish. As I writhed under it, I would at times feel that learning to read had been a curse rather than a blessing. It had given me a view of my wretched condition, without the remedy. It opened my eyes to the horrible pit, but to no ladder upon which to get out. In moments of agony, I envied my fellow-slaves for their stupidity. I have often wished myself a beast. I preferred the condition of the meanest reptile to my own. Any thing, no matter what, to get rid of thinking! It was this everlasting thinking of my condition that tormented me. There was no getting rid of it. It was pressed upon me by every object within sight or hearing, animate or inanimate. The silver trump of freedom had roused my soul to eternal wakefulness. Freedom now appeared, to disappear no more forever. It was heard in every sound, and seen in every thing. It was ever present to torment me with a sense of my wretched condition. I saw nothing without seeing it, I heard nothing without hearing it, and felt nothing without feeling. It looked from every star, it smiled in every calm, breathed in every wind, and moved in every storm.

1. Why does learning to read cause Douglass to perceive his "wretched condition" in everything he experiences?

2. Does Douglass mean to imply that a mental awareness of the injustice of slavery was more intolerable than the physical brutality he suffered as a slave?

3. Why does Douglass use the passive voice to describe the results of being able to think of his "condition" and to conceive of freedom?

4. Why does Douglass describe freedom as a "silver trump" that had roused his soul to "eternal wakefulness"?

5. Why does Douglass describe freedom as an active force, "ever present to torment me with a sense of my wretched condition"?

Passage 4

If my poor old grandmother now lives, she lives to suffer in utter loneliness; she lives to remember and mourn over the loss of children, the loss of grand-children, and the loss of great-grandchildren. They are, in the language of the slave's poet, Whittier,—

> "Gone, gone, sold and gone
> To the rice swamp dank and lone,
> Where the slave-whip ceaseless swings,
> Where the noisome insect stings,
> Where the fever-demon strews
> Poison with the falling dews,
> Where the sickly sunbeams glare
> Through the hot and misty air:—
>   Gone, gone, sold and gone
>   To the rice swamp dank and lone,
>   From Virginia hills and waters—
>   Woe is me, my stolen daughters!"

The hearth is desolate. The children, the unconscious children, who once sang and danced in her presence, are gone. She gropes her way, in the darkness of age, for a drink of water. Instead of the voices of her children, she hears by day the moans of the dove, and by night the screams of the hideous owl. All is gloom. The grave is at the door. And now, when weighed down by the pains and aches of old age, when the head inclines to the feet, when the beginning and ending of human existence meet, and helpless infancy and painful old age combine together—at this time, this most needful time, the time for the exer-cise of that tenderness and affection which children only can exercise toward a declining parent—my poor old grandmother, the devoted mother of twelve children, is left all alone, in yonder little hut, before a few dim embers. She stands—she sits—she staggers—she falls—she groans—she dies—and there are none of her children or grandchildren present, to wipe from her wrinkled brow the cold sweat of death, or to place beneath the sod her fallen remains. Will not a righteous God visit for these things?

1. In telling the story of his grandmother, what techniques does Douglass use to arouse the reader's sympathy?

2. Why does Douglass describe the children as "unconscious"? What are they not conscious of?

3. What effect does Douglass achieve by describing his grandmother's death using short, grammatically repetitive phrases: "She stands—she sits—she staggers—she falls—she groans—she dies"?

4. Douglass ends the story of his grandmother by saying, "Will not a righteous God visit for these things?" Why does Douglass express his desire for justice concerning the death of his grandmother in language that alludes to the Bible?

5. Why, in this work of nonfiction, does Douglass portray in such detail a scene he has only imagined?

Passage 5

Our house stood within a few rods of the Chesapeake Bay, whose broad bosom was ever white with sails from every quarter of the habitable globe. Those beautiful vessels, robed in purest white, so delightful to the eye of freemen, were to me so many shrouded ghosts, to terrify and torment me with thoughts of my wretched condition. I have often, in the deep stillness of a summer's Sabbath, stood all alone upon the lofty banks of that noble bay, and traced, with saddened heart and tearful eye, the countless number of sails moving off to the mighty ocean. The sight of these always affected me powerfully. My thoughts would compel utterance; and there, with no audience but the Almighty, I would pour out my soul's complaint, in my rude way, with an apostrophe to the moving multitude of ships:—

"You are loosed from your moorings, and are free; I am fast in my chains, and am a slave! You move merrily before the gentle gale, and I sadly before the bloody whip! You are freedom's swift-winged angels, that fly round the world; I am confined in bands of iron! O that I were free! O, that I were on one of your gallant decks, and under your protecting wing! Alas! betwixt me and you, the turbid waters roll. Go on, go on. O that I could also go! Could I but swim! If I could fly! O, why was I born a man, of whom to make a brute! The glad ship is gone; she hides in the dim distance. I am left in the hottest hell of unending slavery. O God, save me! God, deliver me! Let me be free! Is there any God? Why am I a slave? I will run away. I will not stand it. Get caught, or get clear, I'll try it. I had as well die with ague as the fever. I have only one life to lose. I had as well be killed running as die standing. Only think of it; one hundred miles straight north, and I am free! Try it? Yes! God helping me, I will. It cannot be that I shall live and die a slave. I will take to the water. This very bay shall yet bear me into freedom. The steamboats steered in a north-east course from North Point. I will do the same; and when I get to the head of the bay, I will turn my canoe adrift, and walk straight through Delaware into Pennsylvania. When I get there, I shall not be required to have a pass; I can travel without being disturbed. Let but the first opportunity offer, and, come what will, I am off. Meanwhile, I will try to bear up under the yoke. I am not the only slave in the world. Why should I fret? I can bear as much as any of them. Besides, I am but a boy, and all boys are bound to some one. It may be that my misery in slavery will only increase my happiness when I get free. There is a better day coming."

1. Why does Douglass personify Chesapeake Bay by referring to its "broad bosom"?

2. Why does Douglass present his thoughts upon seeing the ships in Chesapeake Bay as an address spoken directly to them? What emotion do his words primarily convey?

3. Why do the ships in Chesapeake Bay impress Douglass as emblems of freedom?

4. Why does Douglass think to himself, "I am not the only slave in the world"? What does he gain from knowing that he is one of many?

5. What does Douglass mean when he says, "Besides, I am but a boy, and all boys are bound to some one"? Why does this thought comfort him?

6. Why does Douglass's address to the ships and to God lead him to conclude, "There is a better day coming"?

Passage 6

This battle with Mr. Covey was the turning-point in my career as a slave. It rekindled the few expiring embers of freedom, and revived within me a sense of my own manhood. It recalled the departed self-confidence, and inspired me again with a determination to be free. The gratification afforded by the triumph was a full compensation for whatever else might follow, even death itself. He only can understand the deep satisfaction which I experienced, who has himself repelled by force the bloody arm of slavery. I felt as I never felt before. It was a glorious resurrection, from the tomb of slavery, to the heaven of freedom. My long-crushed spirit rose, cowardice departed, bold defiance took its place; and I now resolved that, however long I might remain a slave in form, the day had passed forever when I could be a slave in fact. I did not hesitate to let it be known of me, that the white man who expected to succeed in whipping, must also succeed in killing me.

From this time I was never again what might be called fairly whipped, though I remained a slave four years afterwards. I had several fights, but was never whipped.

1. Why does his fight with Mr. Covey revive Douglass's sense of "manhood"? Why does it renew his determination to be free?

2. Why does Douglass believe that his triumph over Mr. Covey compensated for "whatever else might follow, even death itself"?

3. What does Douglass mean when, after describing his battle with Mr. Covey, he writes that "however long I might remain a slave in form, the day had passed forever when I could be a slave in fact"?

Passage 7

At times we were almost disposed to give up, and try to content ourselves with our wretched lot; at others, we were firm and unbending in our determination to go. Whenever we suggested any plan, there was shrinking—the odds were fearful. Our path was beset with the greatest obstacles; and if we succeeded in gaining the end of it, our right to be free was yet questionable—we were yet liable to be returned to bondage. We could see no spot, this side of the ocean, where we could be free. We knew nothing about Canada. Our knowledge of the north did not extend farther than New York; and to go there, and be forever harassed with the frightful liability of being returned to slavery—with the certainty of being treated tenfold worse than before—the thought was truly a horrible one, and one which it was not easy to overcome. The case sometimes stood thus: At every gate through which we were to pass, we saw a watchman— at every ferry a guard—on every bridge a sentinel—and in every wood a patrol. We were hemmed in upon every side. Here were the difficulties, real or imagined—the good to be sought, and the evil to be shunned. On the one hand, there stood slavery, a stern reality, glaring frightfully upon us,—its robes already crimsoned with the blood of millions, and even now feasting itself greedily upon our own flesh. On the other hand, away back in the dim distance, under the flickering light of the north star, behind some craggy hill or snow-covered mountain, stood a doubtful freedom—half frozen—beckoning us to come and share its hospitality. This in itself was sometimes enough to stagger us; but when we permitted ourselves to survey the road, we were frequently appalled. Upon either side we saw grim death, assuming the most horrid shapes. Now it was starvation, causing us to eat our own flesh;—now we were contending with the waves, and were drowned;—now we were overtaken, and torn to pieces by the fangs of the terrible bloodhound. We were stung by scorpions, chased by wild beasts, bitten by snakes, and finally, after having nearly reached the desired spot,—after swimming rivers, encountering wild beasts, sleeping in the woods, suffering hunger and nakedness,—we were overtaken by our pursuers, and, in our resistance, we were shot dead upon the spot! I say, this picture sometimes appalled us, and made us

> "rather bear those ills we had,
> Than fly to others, that we knew not of." *

In coming to a fixed determination to run away, we did more than Patrick Henry, when he resolved upon liberty or death. With us it was a doubtful liberty at most, and almost certain death if we failed. For my part, I should prefer death to hopeless bondage.

1. In describing his prospects for escape, why does Douglass personify both slavery and freedom?

2. Why does Douglass describe the "doubtful freedom" that awaits him as "half frozen"?

3. Why does Douglass vividly describe the horrible scenarios that he and his fellow slaves imagined when planning their escape?

4. Why does Douglass quote Shakespeare and Patrick Henry when explaining what he thought while planning to escape? Why does Douglass compare himself and his fellow slaves to Patrick Henry?

5. Why does Douglass include this account of his failed escape attempt in the *Narrative*?

---

* [Shakespeare, *Hamlet* 3.1 81–82.—Eds.]

Passage 8

I have been frequently asked how I felt when I found myself in a free State. I have never been able to answer the question with any satisfaction to myself. It was a moment of the highest excitement I ever experienced. I suppose I felt as one may imagine the unarmed mariner to feel when he is rescued by a friendly man-of-war from the pursuit of a pirate. In writing to a dear friend, immediately after my arrival at New York, I said I felt like one who had escaped a den of hungry lions. This state of mind, however, very soon subsided; and I was again seized with a feeling of great insecurity and loneliness. I was yet liable to be taken back, and subjected to all the tortures of slavery. This in itself was enough to damp the ardor of my enthusiasm. But the loneliness overcame me. There I was in the midst of thousands, and yet a perfect stranger; without home and without friends, in the midst of thousands of my own brethren—children of a common Father, and yet I dared not to unfold to any one of them my sad condition. I was afraid to speak to any one for fear of speaking to the wrong one, and thereby falling into the hands of money-loving kidnappers, whose business it was to lie in wait for the panting fugitive, as the ferocious beasts of the forest lie in wait for their prey. The motto which I adopted when I started from slavery was this—"Trust no man!" I saw in every white man an enemy, and in almost every colored man cause for distrust. It was a most painful situation; and, to understand it, one must needs experience it, or imagine himself in similar circumstances. Let him be a fugitive slave in a strange land—a land given up to be the hunting-ground for slaveholders—whose inhabitants are legalized kidnappers—where he is every moment subjected to the terrible liability of being seized upon by his fellow-men, as the hideous crocodile seizes upon his prey!—I say, let him place himself in my situation—without home or friends— without money or credit—wanting shelter, and no one to give it—wanting bread, and no money to buy it,—and at the same time let him feel that he is pursued by merciless men-hunters, and in total darkness as to what to do, where to go, or where to stay,—perfectly helpless both as to the means of defence and means of escape,—in the midst of plenty, yet suffering the terrible gnawings of hunger,—in the midst of houses, yet having no home,—among fellow-men, yet feeling as if in the midst of wild beasts, whose greediness to swallow up the trembling and half-famished fugitive is only equalled by that with which the monsters of the deep swallow up the helpless fish upon which they subsist,—I say, let him be placed in this most trying situation,—the situation in which I was placed,—then, and not till then, will he fully appreciate the hardships of, and know how to sympathize with, the toil-worn and whip-scarred fugitive slave.

1. Why has Douglass never been satisfied by the answers he has given to how he felt once he was free?

2. At the time he is writing the *Narrative,* how does Douglass seem to feel about having adopted "Trust no man!" as his motto once he had escaped slavery?

3. Why does Douglass repeatedly compare humans to predatory animals when depicting the dangers he faced even after he had gained his freedom?

4. When urging the reader to imagine the situation of a fugitive slave, why does Douglass use such a long sentence, with multiple clauses set off by dashes, to describe the conditions he endured?

NARRATIVE OF THE LIFE OF FREDERICK DOUGLASS

Suggestions for Writing

*Writing about literature is best thought of as an extension of reading
and discussion, as readers return to unresolved questions or investigate unexplored
avenues of inquiry. Readers may also learn and retain more by articulating
their ideas carefully and thoroughly in written form.*

Analytical Writing

1. Does Douglass intend us to see him as an extraordinary person, or as a representative man responding to slavery's injustices?

2. To what extent does Douglass control his own destiny? To what extent does he benefit from "providence" or good luck?

3. In describing the conditions of slavery, Douglass shows not only how slaves were treated like animals, but also how such treatment made it difficult, if not impossible, for slaves to think of themselves as human. Analyze the *Narrative* in terms of what it says about what makes us human.

4. Analyze the role of reading and writing in Douglass's attainment of freedom.

5. Analyze the place of religion in the *Narrative*. How does religion affect the way Douglass views his masters and himself? How does it affect slaveholders? Does the *Narrative* ultimately cast religious faith in a positive or a negative light?

6. What aspects of Douglass's character are most responsible for his survival while a slave and for his eventual escape to freedom?

7. Analyze the portrayal of women in the *Narrative*. Does it differ from the portrayal of men? Does Douglass apply different standards to women than he does to men?

8. Analyze the portrayal of whites in the *Narrative*. What qualities in whites does Douglass praise? What qualities does he most strongly condemn?

Creative/Personal Writing

1. Douglass changed his thinking about slavery after he read a dialogue between a master and his slave in *The Columbian Orator* (reprinted on p. 71). Reflect on a time when you read something that changed the way you thought about a particular topic. How did you think about the topic before and after?

2. Write a dialogue between Douglass and Martin Luther King Jr. in which they tell each other about the causes they struggled for and the obstacles they faced.

3. Write and present a speech in which you call attention to a social, political, or economic injustice.

4. Write two reviews of the *Narrative*—one from the point of view of an abolitionist and one from the point of view of a slaveholder.

Topics for Research

1. Read *Incidents in the Life of a Slave Girl* by Harriet A. Jacobs. How is it different from the *Narrative* in its portrayal of the experience of slavery? To what extent is the fact that it was written by a woman responsible for these differences?

2. Read Martin Luther King Jr.'s "I Have a Dream" speech. Compare its arguments and rhetorical strategies to Douglass's "What to the Slave Is the Fourth of July?"

3. Read *Uncle Tom's Cabin* by Harriet Beecher Stowe. Compared to the *Narrative,* how effective is it in depicting the suffering that slaves endured?

4. Research the Underground Railroad. How effective was it in helping slaves attain their freedom? What dangers did it pose for both slaves and those who tried to assist them?

Background and Context

The following selections offer additional perspectives on slavery in the United States, including the views of other slaves, abolitionists, a slaveholder, and an apologist. They also offer insights into the writing of the *Narrative* and the public life of its author.

ABOVE: This woodcut served as the seal of the Abolition of Slavery Society of England in the 1780s. It later illustrated the American John Greenleaf Whittier's antislavery poem, "Our Countrymen in Chains!" in a broadside published in 1837.

PAGES 68–69: *James Hopkinson's Plantation, Edisto Island, South Carolina* (undated)

First published in 1797, *The Columbian Orator* was a collection of speeches and a standard part of the American school curriculum throughout the first half of the nineteenth century. Douglass purchased the book when he was about twelve years old, and he found this dialogue especially inspiring.

Dialogue Between a Master and Slave

from *The Columbian Orator*

MASTER: Now, villain! What have you to say for this second attempt to run away? Is there any punishment that you do not deserve?

SLAVE: I well know that nothing I can say will avail. I submit to my fate.

MASTER: But are you not a base fellow, a hardened and ungrateful rascal?

SLAVE: I am a slave. That is answer enough.

MASTER: I am not content with that answer. I thought I discerned in you some tokens of a mind superior to your condition. I treated you accordingly. You have been comfortably fed and lodged, not overworked, and attended with the most humane care when you were sick. And is this the return?

SLAVE: Since you condescend to talk with me, as man to man, I will reply. What have you done, what can you do for me, that will compensate for the liberty which you have taken away?

MASTER: I did not take it away. You were a slave when I fairly purchased you.

SLAVE: Did I give my consent to the purchase?

MASTER: You had no consent to give. You had already lost the right of disposing of yourself.

SLAVE: I had lost the power, but how the right? I was treacherously kidnapped in my own country, when following an honest occupation. I was put in chains, sold to one of your countrymen, carried by force on board his ship, brought hither, and exposed to sale like a beast in the market, where you bought me. What step in all this process of violence and injustice can give a *right*? Was it in the villain who stole me, in the slave-merchant who tempted him to do so, or in you who encouraged the slave-merchant to bring his cargo of human cattle to cultivate your lands?

MASTER: It is in the order of Providence that one man should become subservient to another. It ever has been so, and ever will be. I found the custom, and did not make it.

SLAVE: You cannot but be sensible, that the robber who puts a pistol to your breast may make just the same plea. Providence gives him a power over your life and property; it gave my enemies a power over my liberty. But it has also given me legs to escape with, and what should prevent me from using them? Nay, what should restrain me from retaliating the wrongs I have suffered, if a favorable occasion should offer?

MASTER: Gratitude! I repeat, gratitude! Have I not endeavored ever since I possessed you to alleviate your misfortunes by kind treatment, and does that confer no obligation? Consider how much worse your condition might have been under another master.

SLAVE: You have done nothing for me more than for your working cattle. Are they not well fed and tended? Do you work them harder than your slaves? Is not the rule of treating both designed only for your own advantage? You treat both your men and beast slaves better than some of your neighbors, because you are more prudent and wealthy than they.

MASTER: You might add more humane, too.

SLAVE: Humane! Does it deserve that apellation to keep your fellow men in forced subjection, deprived of all exercise of their free will, liable to all the injuries that your own caprice or the brutality of your overseers may heap on them, and devoted, soul and body, only to your pleasure and emolument? Can gratitude take place between creatures in such a state and the tyrant who holds them in it? Look at these limbs; are they not those of a man? Think that I have the spirit of a man, too.

MASTER: But it was my intention not only to make your life tolerably comfortable at present, but to provide for you in your old age.

SLAVE: Alas! Is a life like mine, torn from country, friends, and all I held dear, and compelled to toil under the burning sun for a master, worth thinking about for old age? No; the sooner it ends, the sooner I shall obtain that relief for which my soul pants.

MASTER: Is it impossible then, to hold you by any ties but those of constraint and severity?

SLAVE: It is impossible to make one who has felt the value of freedom acquiesce in being a slave.

MASTER: Suppose I were to restore you to your liberty, would you reckon that a favor?

SLAVE: The greatest; for although it would only be undo-
ing a wrong, I know too well how few among
mankind are capable of sacrificing interest to
justice, not to prize the exertion when it is made.

MASTER: I do it, then; be free.

SLAVE: Now I am indeed your servant, though not your
slave. And as the first return I can make for your
kindness, I will tell you freely the condition in
which you live. You are surrounded with impla-
cable foes, who long for a safe opportunity to
revenge upon you and the other planters all the
miseries they have endured. The more generous
their natures, the more indignant they feel against
that cruel injustice which has dragged them hither
and doomed them to perpetual servitude. You can
rely on no kindness on your part to soften the
obduracy of their resentment. You have reduced
them to the state of brute beasts; and if they have
not the stupidity of beasts of burden, they must
have the ferocity of beasts of prey. Superior force
alone can give you security. As soon as that fails,
you are at the mercy of the merciless. Such is the
social bond between master and slave!

Although its creator is unknown,
this image of a supplicant female
slave was first used in 1826 by the
Ladies Negro's Friend Society of
Birmingham, England. In the 1830s,
the image became the emblem of a
movement led by American women
opposed to slavery.

A List Women their ages & value

Names	Ages	Full Hands	Half Hands	Value	Remarks
Letha	30 years	"		500 00	good hand
Elmira	25 "		½	400 00	sickly
Eliza Ann	18 "	"		500 00	good hand
Nanny	16 "	"		500 00	good hand
Long Mariah	45 "		½	300 00	not much account
Tena	40 "	"		400 00	well disposed fair hand
Eliza	30 "	"		400 00	fair hand
Amy	35 "	"		400 00	fair hand
Jeanette	35 "	"		400 00	very good cook
Peggy	30 "	"		500 00	good hand
Fanny	18 "	"		500 00	good hand
Nancy	16 "	"		500 00	good hand
Harriet (Black)	25 "	"		500 00	good hand
Olive	20 "	"		500 00	good hand
Hager	50 "		½	300 00	excellent in telling lies
Angelina	30 "	"		400 00	very good hand
Mariah cook.	40 "	"		300 00	all mouth, plantation cook
Polly	40 "	"		300 00	very Bad woman, great temper
Lucy	30 "	"		500 00	good hand
Martha	35 "	"		500 00	good hand
Lydia	35 "	"		400 00	good hand
Yellow Harriet	18 "		¼	100 00	very little account sickly
Catherine	30 "	"		400 00	fair hand
Penelope	50 "		¼	300 00	Plantation nurse
				9500 00	

Inventory of slaves, including their ages and values,
on the Wilton plantation in Louisiana in 1849

The Old Plantation (late eighteenth century) by an unknown painter

Slaves produced an enormous variety of musical expression. These songs suggest the harsh conditions in which slaves lived, as well as their aspirations for release and freedom. "Me and My Captain," "Blue Tail Fly," and "All the Pretty Little Horses" convey the bitterness slaves felt toward their masters. "Follow the Drinking Gourd" gave direction to slaves traveling on the Underground Railroad, the network of people and hiding places that helped tens of thousands of slaves escape the South in the decades prior to the Civil War. The "drinking gourd" is another name for the Big Dipper, which pointed the way north to freedom. "Go Down, Moses" may have been about one of the Railroad's most famous "conductors," an escaped slave named Harriet Tubman.

Slave Songs

Me and My Captain

Me and captain don't agree,
But he don't know, 'cause he don't ask me;
He don't know, he don't know my mind,
When he see me laughing
Just laughing to keep from crying.

Oh, what's the matter now,
Me and my captain can't get along nohow;
He don't know, he don't know my mind,
When he see me laughing
Just laughing to keep from crying.

He call me low down I just laugh,
Kick seat of my pants and that ain't half;
He don't know, he don't know my mind,
When he see me laughing
Just laughing to keep from crying.

Got one mind for white folks to see,
'Nother for what I know is me;
He don't know, he don't know my mind,
When he see me laughing
Just laughing to keep from crying.

Blue Tail Fly

When I was young I use to wait
On Master and give him his plate,
And pass the bottle when he got dry,
And brush away the blue tail fly.

Chorus:
    Jimmy crack corn and I don't care,
    Jimmy crack corn and I don't care,
    Jimmy crack corn and I don't care,
      My master's gone away.

When he ride in the afternoon,
I follow him with a hickory broom;
The pony being rather shy
When bitten by a blue tail fly.

One day he ride around the farm,
The flies so numerous they did swarm;
One chanced to bite him on the thigh—
The devil take the blue tail fly.

The pony run, he jump, he pitch;
He tumble Master in the ditch.
He died and the jury wondered why—
The verdict was the blue tail fly.

They laid him under a 'simmon tree;
His epitaph is there to see:
"Beneath this stone I'm forced to lie,
A victim of the blue tail fly."

Old Master's gone, now let him rest,
They say all things are for the best;
I'll never forget, till the day I die,
Old Master and that blue tail fly.

On de No'thern Road (1926)
by Aaron Douglas

78

All the Pretty Little Horses

Hushaby, don't you cry,
Go to sleepy, little baby.
When you wake, you shall have cake,
And all the pretty little horses.
Blacks and bays, dapples and grays,
Coach and six-a little horses.
    Way down yonder in the meadow,
    There's a poor little lambie;
    The bees and the butterflies pickin' out his eyes,
    The poor little thing cries, "Mammy."
Hushaby, don't you cry,
Go to sleepy, little baby.

I couldn't hear nobody pray
(1925) by Aaron Douglas

79

Follow the Drinking Gourd

Follow the drinking gourd,
Follow the drinking gourd,
For the old man is a-waiting
For to carry you to freedom,
Follow the drinking gourd.

Forest Fear (1926)
by Aaron Douglas

Go Down, Moses

When Israel was in Egypt's land,
    Let my people go;
Oppressed so hard they could not stand,
    Let my people go.

Chorus:
    Go down, Moses, way down
        in Egypt's land;
    Tell old Pharoah, to let my people go.

Thus saith the Lord, bold Moses said,
    Let my people go;
If not I'll smite your first born dead,
    Let my people go.

No more shall they in bondage toil,
    Let my people go;
Let them come out with Egypt's spoil,
    Let my people go.

O 'twas a dark and dismal night,
    Let my people go;
When Moses led the Israelites,
    Let my people go.

The Lord told Moses what to do,
    Let my people go;
To lead the children of Israel through,
    Let my people go.

O come along, Moses, you won't get lost,
    Let my people go;
Stretch out your rod and come across,
    Let my people go.

As Israel stood by the water side,
    Let my people go;
At the command of God it did divide,
    Let my people go.

And when they reached the other side,
    Let my people go;
They sang a song of triumph o'er,
    Let my people go.

You won't get lost in the wilderness,
    Let my people go;
With a lighted candle in your breast,
    Let my people go.

O let us all from bondage flee,
    Let my people go;
And let us all in Christ be free,
    Let my people go.

We need not always weep and moan,
    Let my people go;
And wear these slavery chains forlorn,
    Let my people go.

What a beautiful morning that will be,
    Let my people go;
When time breaks up in eternity,
    Let my people go.

Watching the Good Trains Go By (1964) by Romare Bearden

This selection comes from *Incidents in the Life of a Slave Girl* (1861), the first slave narrative written by a woman. The author, Harriet A. Jacobs (ca. 1813–1897), used the name "Linda Brent" to conceal her identity as the subject and author of her story. Because of its perspective on the plight of female slaves in particular, Jacobs's book became an important work of both African American and American women's literature.

The Trials of Girlhood

Harriet A. Jacobs

During the first years of my service in Dr. Flint's family, I was accustomed to share some indulgences with the children of my mistress. Though this seemed to me no more than right, I was grateful for it, and tried to merit the kindness by the faithful discharge of my duties. But I now entered on my fifteenth year— a sad epoch in the life of a slave girl. My master began to whisper foul words in my ear. Young as I was, I could not remain ignorant of their import. I tried to treat them with indifference or contempt. The master's age, my extreme youth, and the fear that his conduct would be reported to my grandmother, made him bear this treatment for many months. He was a crafty man, and resorted to many means to accomplish his purposes. Sometimes he had stormy, terrific ways that made his victims tremble; sometimes he assumed a gentleness that he thought must surely subdue. Of the two, I preferred his stormy moods, although they left me trembling. He tried his utmost to corrupt the pure principles my grandmother had instilled. He peopled my young mind with unclean images, such as only a vile monster could think of. I turned from him with disgust and hatred. But he was my master. I was compelled to live under the same roof with him—where I saw a man forty years my senior daily violating the most sacred commandments of nature. He told me I was his property; that I must be subject to his will in all things. My soul revolted against the mean tyranny. But where could I turn for protection? No matter whether the slave girl be as black as ebony or as fair as her mistress. In either case, there is no shadow of law to protect her from insult, from violence, or even from death; all these are inflicted by fiends who bear the shape of men. The mistress, who ought to protect the helpless victim, has no other feelings toward her but those of jealousy and rage. The degradation, the wrongs, the vices, that grow out of slavery, are more than I can describe. They are greater than you would willingly believe. Surely, if you credited one half the truths that are told you concerning the helpless millions suffering in this cruel bondage, you at the north would not help to tighten the yoke. You surely would refuse to do for the master, on your own soil, the mean and cruel work which trained bloodhounds and the lowest class of whites do for him at the south.

Everywhere the years bring to all enough of sin and sorrow; but in slavery the very dawn of life is darkened by these shadows. Even the little child, who is accustomed to wait on her mistress and her children, will learn, before she is twelve years old, why it is that her mistress hates such and such a one among the slaves. Perhaps the child's own mother is among those hated ones. She listens to violent outbreaks of jealous passion, and cannot help understanding what is the cause. She will become prematurely knowing in evil things. Soon she will learn to tremble when she hears her

$100 REWARD

WILL be given for the apprehension and delivery of my Servant Girl HARRIET. She is a light mulatto, 21 years of age, about 5 feet 4 inches high, of a thick and corpulent habit, having on her head a thick covering of black hair that curls naturally, but which can be easily combed straight. She speaks easily and fluently, and has an agreeable carriage and address. Being a good seamstress, she has been accustomed to dress well, has a variety of very fine clothes, made in the prevailing fashion, and will probably appear, if abroad, tricked out in gay and fashionable finery. As this girl absconded from the plantation of my son without any known cause or provocation, it is probable she designs to transport herself to the North.

The above reward, with all reasonable charges, will be given for apprehending her, or securing her in any prison or jail within the U. States.

All persons are hereby forewarned against harboring or entertaining her, or being in any way instrumental in her escape, under the most rigorous penalties of the law.
JAMES NORCOM.
Edenton, N. C. June 30

Notice for runaway Harriet Jacobs placed by her owner, Dr. James Norcom, in the *American Beacon* in 1835

master's footfall. She will be compelled to realize that she is no longer a child. If God has bestowed beauty upon her, it will prove her greatest curse. That which commands admiration in the white woman only hastens the degradation of the female slave. I know that some are too much brutalized by slavery to feel the humiliation of their position; but many slaves feel it most acutely, and shrink from the memory of it. I cannot tell how much I suffered in the presence of these wrongs, nor how I am still pained by the retrospect. My master met me at every turn, reminding me that I belonged to him, and swearing by heaven and earth that he would compel me to submit to him. If I went out for a breath of fresh air, after a day of unwearied toil, his footsteps dogged me. If I knelt by my mother's grave, his dark shadow fell on me even there. The light heart which nature had given me became heavy with sad forebodings. The other slaves in my master's house noticed the change. Many of them pitied me; but none dared to ask the cause. They had no need to inquire. They knew too well the guilty practices under that roof; and they were aware that to speak of them was an offence that never went unpunished.

I longed for someone to confide in. I would have given the world to have laid my head on my grandmother's faithful bosom, and told her all my troubles. But Dr. Flint swore he would kill me, if I was not as silent as the grave. Then, although my grandmother was all in all to me, I feared her as well as loved her. I had been accustomed to look up to her with a respect bordering upon awe. I was very young, and felt shamefaced about telling her such impure things, especially as I knew her to be very strict on such subjects. Moreover, she was a woman of a high spirit. She was usually very quiet in her demeanor; but if her indignation was once roused, it was not very easily quelled. I had been told that she once chased a white gentleman with a loaded pistol, because he insulted one of her daughters. I dreaded the consequences of a violent outbreak; and both pride and fear kept me silent. But though I did not confide in my grandmother, and even evaded her vigilant watchfulness and inquiry, her presence in the neighborhood was some protection to me. Though she had been a slave, Dr. Flint was afraid of her. He dreaded her scorching rebukes. Moreover, she was known and patronized by many people; and he did not wish to have his villainy made public. It was lucky for me that I did not live on a distant plantation, but in a town not so large that the inhabitants were ignorant of each other's affairs. Bad as are the laws and customs in a slaveholding community, the doctor, as a professional man, deemed it prudent to keep up some outward show of decency.

O, what days and nights of fear and sorrow that man caused me! Reader, it is not to awaken sympathy for myself that I am telling you truthfully what I suffered in slavery. I do it to kindle a flame of compassion in your hearts for my sisters who are still in bondage, suffering as I once suffered.

I once saw two beautiful children playing together. One was a fair white child; the other was her slave, and also her sister. When I saw them embracing each other, and heard their joyous laughter, I turned sadly away from the lovely sight. I foresaw the inevitable blight that would fall on the little slave's heart. I knew how soon her laughter would be changed to sighs. The fair child grew up to be a still fairer woman. From childhood to womanhood her pathway was blooming with flowers, and overarched by a sunny sky. Scarcely one day of her life had been clouded when the sun rose on her happy bridal morning.

How had those years dealt with her slave sister, the little playmate of her childhood? She, also, was very beautiful; but the flowers and sunshine of love were not for her. She drank the cup of sin, and shame, and misery, whereof her persecuted race are compelled to drink.

In view of these things, why are ye silent, ye free men and women of the north? Why do your tongues falter in maintenance of the right? Would that I had more ability! But my heart is so full, and my pen is so weak! There are noble men and women who plead for us, striving to help those who cannot help themselves. God bless them! God give them strength and courage to go on! God bless those, everywhere, who are laboring to advance the cause of humanity!

Harriet Jacobs in 1894

THE

CONFESSIONS

OF

NAT TURNER,

THE LEADER OF THE LATE

INSURRECTION IN SOUTHAMPTON, VA.

As fully and voluntarily made to

THOMAS R. GRAY,

In the prison where he was confined, and acknowledged by
him to be such when read before the Court of Southampton; with the certificate, under seal of
the Court convened at Jerusalem,
Nov. 5, 1831, for his trial.

ALSO, AN AUTHENTIC

ACCOUNT OF THE WHOLE INSURRECTION,

WITH LISTS OF THE WHITES WHO WERE MURDERED,

AND OF THE NEGROES BROUGHT BEFORE THE COURT OF
SOUTHAMPTON, AND THERE SENTENCED, &c.

Peter L. Storm

Baltimore:
PUBLISHED BY THOMAS R. GRAY.
Lucas & Deaver, print.
1831.

Nat Turner (1800–1831), a slave and preacher, led the most famous of the Southern slave revolts. On August 21, 1831, Turner and about seventy other slaves killed about sixty white Virginians over the course of forty hours. At least one hundred slaves were killed in retaliation, and Turner was captured, tried, and hanged, along with others accused of participating in the rebellion. Turner dictated his confession to Thomas R. Gray, his court-appointed attorney.

Confession

(SELECTION)

Nat Turner

Agreeable to his own appointment, on the evening he was committed to prison, with permission of the jailer, I visited Nat on Tuesday the first of November, when, without being questioned at all, he commenced his narrative in the following words:

Sir, you have asked me to give a history of the motives which induced me to undertake the late insurrection, as you call it. To do so I must go back to the days of my infancy, and even before I was born. I was thirty-one years of age the second of October last and born the property of Benjamin Turner, of this county. In my childhood a circumstance occurred which made an indelible impression on my mind and laid the groundwork of that enthusiasm which has terminated so fatally to many, both white and black, and for which I am about to atone at the gallows. It is here necessary to relate this circumstance, trifling as it may seem; it was the commencement of that belief which has grown with time, and even now, sir, in this dungeon, helpless and forsaken as I am, I cannot divest myself of. Being at play with other children, when three or four years old, I was telling them something, which my mother overhearing, said it had happened before I was born. I stuck to my story, however, and related some things which went, in her opinion to confirm it; others being called on were greatly astonished, knowing that these things had happened, and caused them to say in my hearing, I surely would be a prophet, as the Lord had shown me things that had happened before my birth. And my father and mother strengthened me in this my first impression, saying in my presence, I was intended for some great purpose, which they had always thought from certain marks on my head and breast [a parcel of excrescences which I believe not at all uncommon, particularly among Negroes, as I have seen several with the same. In this case he has either cut them off or they have nearly disappeared].

My grandmother, who was very religious and to whom I was much attached, my master, who belonged to the church, and other religious persons who visited the house, and whom I often saw at prayers, noticing the singularity of my manners, I suppose, and my uncommon intelligence for a child, remarked I had too much sense to be raised and if I was, I would never be of any service to anyone as a slave. To a mind like mine, restless, inquisitive, and observant of everything that was passing, it is easy to suppose that religion was the subject to which it would be directed, and although this subject principally occupied my thoughts, there was nothing that I saw or heard of to which my attention was not directed. The manner in which I learned to read and write not only had great influence on my own mind, as I acquired it with the most perfect ease, so much so that I have no recollection whatever of learning the alphabet, but to the astonishment of the family, one day, when a book was shown to me to keep me from crying, I began spelling the names of different objects. This was a source of wonder to all in the neighborhood, particularly the blacks, and this learning was constantly improved at all opportunities. When I got large enough to go to work, while employed, I was reflecting on many things that would present themselves to my imagination, and whenever an opportunity occurred of looking at a book, when the schoolchildren were getting their lessons, I would find many things that the fertility of my own imagination had depicted to me before; all my time not devoted to my master's service was spent either in prayer, or in making experiments in casting different things in molds made of earth, in attempting to make paper, gunpowder, and many other experiments that, although I could not perfect, yet convinced me of its practicability if I had the means.

I was not addicted to stealing in my youth, nor have ever been. Yet such was the confidence of the Negroes in the neighborhood, even at this early period of my life, in my superior judgment, that they would often carry me with them when they were going on any roguery, to plan for them. Growing up among them, with this confidence in my superior judgment, and when this, in their opinions, was perfected by divine inspiration, from the circumstances already alluded to in my infancy, and which belief was ever afterward zealously inculcated by the austerity of my life and manners, which became the subject of remark with white and black.

Having soon discovered to be great, I must appear so and, therefore, studiously avoided mixing in society and wrapped myself in mystery, devoting my time to fasting and prayer. By this time, having arrived to man's estate and hearing the scriptures commented on at meetings, I was struck with that particular passage which says: "Seek ye the kingdom of Heaven and all things shall be added unto you." I reflected much on this passage and prayed daily for light on this subject. As I was praying one day at my plow, the Spirit spoke to me, saying "Seek ye the kingdom of Heaven and all things shall be added unto you."

QUESTION: What do you mean by the Spirit?
ANSWER: The Spirit that spoke to the prophets in former days.

And I was greatly astonished and for two years prayed continually, whenever my duty would permit. And then again I had the same revelation, which fully confirmed me in the impression that I was ordained for some great purpose in the hands of the Almighty.

Several years rolled round, in which many events occurred to strengthen me in this belief. At this time I reverted in my mind to the remarks made of me in my childhood, and the things that had been shown me, and as it had been said of me in my childhood by those by whom I had been taught to pray, both white and black, and in whom I had the greatest confidence, that I had too much sense to be raised, and if I was I would never be of any use to anyone as a slave. Now finding I had arrived to man's estate and was a slave, and these revelations being made known to me, I began to direct my attention to this great object, to fulfill the purpose for which, by this time, I felt assured I was intended. Knowing the influence I had obtained over the minds of my fellow servants (not by the means of conjuring and such like tricks, for to them I always spoke of such things with contempt, but by the communion of the Spirit whose revelations I often communicated to them, and they believed and said my wisdom came from God), I now began to prepare them for my purpose, by telling them something was about to happen that would terminate in fulfilling the great promise that had been made to me.

About this time I was placed under an overseer, from whom I ran away; and after remaining in the woods thirty days, I returned, to the astonishment of the Negroes on the plantation, who thought I had made my escape to some other part of the country, as my father had done before. But the reason of my return was that the Spirit appeared to me and said I had my wishes directed to the things of this world, and not to the kingdom of heaven, and that I should return to the service of my earthly master, "For he who knoweth his Master's will, and doeth it not, shall be beaten with many stripes, and thus have I chastened you." And the Negroes found fault, and murmured against me, saying that if they had my sense they would not serve any master in the world. And about this time I had a vision, and I saw white spirits and black spirits engaged in battle, and the sun was darkened, the thunder rolled in the heavens, and blood flowed in streams, and I heard a voice saying, "Such is your luck, such you are called to see, and let it come rough or smooth, you must surely bear it."

I now withdrew myself as much as my situation would permit from the intercourse of my fellow servants, for the avowed purpose of serving the Spirit more fully, and it appeared to me, and reminded me of the things it had already shown me, and that it would then reveal to me the knowledge of the elements, the revolution of the planets, the operation of tides, and changes of the seasons. After this revelation in the year 1825 and the knowledge of the elements being made known to me, I sought more than ever to obtain true holiness before the great day of judgment should appear, and then I began to receive the true knowledge of faith. And from the first steps of righteousness until the last, was I made perfect; and the Holy Ghost was with me, and said, "Behold me as I stand in the heavens," and I looked and saw the forms of men in different attitudes, and there were lights in the sky to which the children of darkness gave other names than what they really were, for they were the lights of the Savior's hands, stretched forth from east to west, even as they were extended on the cross on Calvary for the redemption of sinners. And I wondered greatly at these miracles, and prayed to be informed of a certainty of the meaning thereof, and shortly afterward, while laboring in the field, I discovered drops of blood on the corn, as though it were dew from heaven, and I communicated it to many, both white and black in the neighborhood. And I then found on the leaves in the woods hieroglyphic characters and numbers, with the forms of men in different attitudes, portrayed in blood, and representing the figures I had seen before in the heavens. And now the Holy Ghost had revealed itself to me and made plain the miracles it had shown me. For as the blood of Christ had been shed on this earth, and had ascended to heaven for the salvation of sinners, and was now returning to earth again in the form of dew, and as the leaves on the trees bore the impression of the figures I had seen in the heavens, it was plain to me that the Savior was about to lay down the yoke he had bourne for the sins of men, and the great day of judgment was at hand.

About this time, I told these things to a white man (Etheldred T. Brantley) on whom it had a wonderful effect, and he ceased from his wickedness and was attacked immediately with a cutaneous eruption, and blood oozed from the pores of his skin, and after praying and fasting nine days he was healed, and the Spirit appeared to me again and said, as the Savior had been baptized, so should we be also; and when the white people would not let us be baptized by the church, we went down into the water together, in the sight of many who reviled us, and were baptized by the Spirit. After this I rejoiced greatly, and gave thanks to God. And on May 12, 1828, I heard a loud noise in the heavens, and the Spirit instantly appeared to me and said the Serpent was loosened, and Christ had laid down the yoke he had borne for the sins of men, and that I should take it on and fight against the Serpent, for the time was fast approaching when the first should be last and the last should be first.

QUESTION: Do you not find yourself mistaken now?
ANSWER: Was not Christ crucified?

And by signs in the heavens that it would make known to me when I should commence the great work, and until the first sign appeared, I should conceal it from the knowledge of men. And on the appearance of the sign (the eclipse of the sun last February), I should arise and prepare myself and slay my enemies with their own weapons. And immediately on the sign appearing in the heavens, the seal was removed from my lips, and I communicated the great work laid out for me to do, to four in whom I had the greatest confidence (Henry, Hark, Nelson, and Sam). It was intended by us to have begun the work of death on the fourth of July last. Many were the plans formed and rejected by us, and it affected my mind to such a degree that I fell sick, and the time passed without our coming to any determination how to commence; still forming new schemes and rejecting them, when the sign appeared again, which determined me not to wait longer.

Since the commencement of 1830, I had been living with Mr. Joseph Travis, who was to me a kind master and placed the greatest confidence in me; in fact, I had no cause to complain of his treatment to me. On Saturday evening, the twentieth of August, it was agreed between Henry, Hark, and myself to prepare a dinner the next day for the men we expected, and then to concert a plan, as

we had not yet determined on any. Hark, on the following morning, brought a pig, and Henry brandy, and being joined by Sam, Nelson, Will, and Jack, they prepared in the woods a dinner, where, about three o'clock, I joined them.

QUESTION: Why were you so backward in joining them?
ANSWER: The same reason that had caused me not to mix with them for
      years before.

I saluted them on coming up and asked Will how came he there; he answered, his life was worth no more than others, and his liberty as dear to him. I asked him if he thought to obtain it? He said he would, or lose his life. This was enough to put him in full confidence. Jack, I knew, was only a tool in the hands of Hark. It was quickly agreed we should commence at home (Mr. J. Travis's) on that night, and until we had armed and equipped ourselves and gathered sufficient force, neither age nor sex was to be spared (which was invariably adhered to).

We remained at the feast until about two hours in the night, when we went to the house and found Austin; they all went to the cider press and drank, except myself. On returning to the house, Hark went to the door with an ax, for the purpose of breaking it open, as we knew we were strong enough to murder the family if they were awaked by the noise; but, reflecting that it might create an alarm in the neighborhood, we determined to enter the house secretly and murder them while sleeping. Hark got a ladder and set it against the chimney on which I ascended and, hoisting a window, entered and came downstairs, unbarred the door, and removed the guns from their places. It was then observed that I must spill the first blood. On which, armed with a hatchet and accompanied by Will, I entered my master's chamber. It being dark, I could not give a death blow; the hatchet glanced from his head; he sprang from the bed and called his wife. It was his last word. Will laid him dead with a blow of his ax, and Mrs. Travis shared the same fate, as she lay in bed.

The murder of this family, five in number, was the work of a moment, not one of them awoke. There was a little infant, sleeping in a cradle, that was forgotten until we had left the house and gone some distance, when Henry and Will returned and killed it. We got here four guns that would shoot and several old muskets, with a pound or two of powder. We remained some time at the barn, where we paraded; I formed them in a line as soldiers and, after carrying them through all the maneuvers I was master of, marched them off to Mr. Salathul Francis's, about 600 yards distant. Sam and Will went to the door and knocked. Mr. Francis asked who was there; Sam replied it was him and he had a letter for him, on which he got up and came to the door. They immediately seized him, and, dragging him out a little from the door, he was dispatched by repeated blows on the head; there was no other white person in the family.

We started from there for Mrs. Reese's, maintaining the most perfect silence on our march, where finding the door unlocked, we entered and murdered Mrs. Reese in her bed, while sleeping. Her son awoke, but it was only to sleep the sleep of death. He had only time to say who is that, and he was no more. From Mrs. Reese's we went to Mrs. Turner's, a mile distant, which we reached about sunrise on Monday morning. Henry, Austin, and Sam went to the still where, finding Mr. Peebles, Austin shot him, and the rest of us went to the house; as we approached, the family discovered us and shut the door. Vain hope! Will, with one stroke of his ax, opened it, and we entered and found Mrs. Turner and Mrs. Newsome in the middle of a room almost frightened to death.

HORRID MASSACRE IN VIRGINIA.

The Scenes which the above Plate is designed to represent, are---Figure 1. a Mother intreating for the lives of her children. ---2. Mr. Travis, cruelly murdered by his own Slaves.---3. Mr. Barrow, who bravely defended himself until his wife escaped. ----4. A company of mounted Dragoons in pursuit of the Blacks.

Just Published, an Authentic and Interesting

NARRATIVE

OF THE

TRAGICAL SCENE

Which was witnessed in Southampton county (Virginia) on Monday the 22d of August last, when FIFTY FIVE of its inhabitants (mostly women and children) were inhumanly massacred by the Blacks!

Short and imperfect sketches of the horrid massacre above mentioned have appeared in the public Journals, but the public are now presented with every particular relative thereto, communicated by those who were eye witnesses of the bloody scene, and confirmed by the confessions of several of the Blacks while under sentence of death.

A more shocking instance of human butchery has seldom occurred in any country, and never before in this—the merciless wretches carried destruction to every white person they found in the houses, whether the hoary head, the lovely virgin, or the sleeping infant in the cradle! they spared none!—a widow (Mrs. Whitehead) and her 10 children were murdered in one house! among the slain on that fatal night, was an amiable young lady but 17 years of age, who the day following was to have been united in marriage to a young gentleman of North-Carolina, who had left home the evening preceding with the expectation of conveying there the succeeding day the object of his affections! but, alas! how sad was his disappointment! he was the third person who entered the house after the horrid massacre, to witness the mangled remains of her whom he was so shortly to espouse! The Blacks after having completed their work of death, attempted to evade the pursuit of those who had collected to oppose them, by secreting themselves in a neighboring swamp, to the borders of which they were pursued by a company of mounted dragoons. Of the fifty five slain nearly two thirds of the number were children, not exceeding twelve years of age! and it was truly a melancholly scene (as was observed to the writer by one who witnessed it) to behold on the day of their interment so great a number of coffins collected, surrounded by the weeping relatives!

While the friends of humanity however or wherever situated, cannot but sincerely and deeply lament the awful destruction of so many innocent lives, yet, the humane and philanthopic citizens of New-England, and of the middle States, cannot feel too thankful for the repose and peace of conscience which they enjoy, by wisely and humanely abolishing laws dooming a free born fellow being (without fault or crime) to perpetual bondage!---an example truly worthy of imitation by our brethren at the South.

The Narrative (which contains every important particular relating to the horrid massacre) is afforded for the trifling sum of 12 1-2 Cents. ☞ This paper left for perusal, and to be returned when called for.

Will immediately killed Mrs. Turner with one blow of his ax. I took Mrs. Newsome by the hand, and with the sword I had when I was apprehended, I struck her several blows over the head, but not being able to kill her, as the sword was dull. Will, turning around and discovering it, dispatched her also.

A general destruction of property and search for money and ammunition always succeeded the murders. By this time my company amounted to fifteen, and nine men mounted, who started for Mrs. Whitehead's (the other six were to go through a byway to Mr. Bryant's and rejoin us at Mrs. Whitehead's). As we approached the house we discovered Mr. Richard Whitehead standing in the cotton patch, near the lane fence; we called him over into the lane, and Will, the executioner, was near at hand, with his fatal ax, to send him to an untimely grave. As we pushed on to the house, I discovered someone run round the garden, and, thinking it was some of the white family, I pursued them, but finding it was a servant girl belonging to the house, I returned to commence the work of death, but they whom I left had not been idle; all the family were already murdered but Mrs. Whitehead and her daughter Margaret. As I came round to the door I saw Will pulling Mrs. Whitehead out of the house, and at the step he nearly severed her head from her body with his broad ax. Miss Margaret, when I discovered her, had concealed herself in the corner formed by the projection of the cellar cap from the house. On my approach she fled, but was soon overtaken, and, after repeated blows with a sword, I killed her by a blow on the head with a fence rail. By this time, the six who had gone by Mr. Bryant's rejoined us and informed me they had done the work of death assigned them.

We again divided, part going to Mr. Richard Porter's, and from thence to Nathaniel Francis's, the others to Mr. Howell Harris's and Mr. T. Doyle's. On my reaching Mr. Porter's, he had escaped with his family. I understood there that the alarm had already spread, and I immediately returned to bring up those sent to Mr. Doyle's and Mr. Howell Harris's; the party I left going on to Mr. Francis's, having told I would join them in that neighborhood. I met these sent to Mr. Doyle's and Harris's returning, having met Mr. Doyle on the road and killed him; and learning from some who joined them that Mr. Harris was from home, I immediately pursued the course taken by the party gone on before; but knowing they would complete the work of death and pillage at Mr. Francis's before I could get there, I went to Mr. Peter Edwards's expecting to find them there, but they had been here also. I then went to Mr. John T. Barrow's; they had been here and murdered him. I pursued on their track to Captain Newit Harris's, where I found the greater part mounted and ready to start. The men, now amounting to about forty, shouted and hurrahed as I rode up; some were in the yard, loading their guns, others drinking. They said Captain Harris and his family had escaped, the property in the house they destroyed, robbing him of money and other valuables.

I ordered them to mount and march instantly; this was about nine or ten o'clock Monday morning. I proceeded to Mr. Levi Waller's, two or three miles distant. I took my station in the rear, and as it was my object to carry terror and devastation wherever we went, I placed fifteen or twenty of the best mounted and most to be relied on in front, who generally approached the houses as fast as their horses could run. This was for two purposes, to prevent their escape and strike terror to the inhabitants. On this account I never got to the houses, after leaving Mrs. Whitehead's, until the murders were committed, except in one case. I sometimes got in sight in time to see the work of death completed, viewed the mangled bodies as they lay, in silent satisfaction, and immediately started in quest of other victims.

Having murdered Mrs. Waller and ten children, we started for Mr. William Williams's; having killed him and two little boys that were there; while engaged in this, Mrs. Williams fled and got some distance from the house, but she was pursued, overtaken, and compelled to get up behind one of the company, who brought her back, and after showing her the mangled body of her lifeless husband, she was told to get down and lay by his side, where she was shot dead. I then started for Mr. Jacob Williams's, where the family were murdered. Here we found a young man named Drury, who had come on business with Mr. Williams; he was pursued, overtaken, and shot. Mrs. Vaughan's was the next place we visited, and, after murdering the family here, I determined on starting for Jerusalem. Our number amounted now to fifty or sixty, all mounted and armed with guns, axes, swords, and clubs.

On reaching Mr. James W. Parker's gate, immediately on the road leading to Jerusalem and about three miles distant, it was proposed to me to call there, but I objected, as I knew he was gone to Jerusalem, and my object was to reach there as soon as possible. But some of the men having relations at Mr. Parker's, it was agreed that they might call and get his people. I remained at the gate on the road with seven or eight; the others going across the field to the house, about half a mile off. After waiting some time for them, I became impatient and started to the house for them, and on our return we were met by a party of white men, who had pursued our bloodstained track, and who had fired on those at the gate and dispersed them, which I knew nothing of, not having been at that time rejoined by any of them.

Immediately on discovering the whites, I ordered my men to halt and form, as they appeared to be alarmed. The white men, eighteen in number, approached us in about one hundred yards, when one of them fired (this was against the positive orders of Captain Alexander P. Peete, who commanded, and who had directed the men to reserve their fire until within thirty paces). And I discovered about half of them retreating. I then ordered my men to fire and rush on them; the few remaining stood their ground until we approached within fifty yards, when they fired and retreated. We pursued and overtook some of them who we thought we left dead (they were not killed); after pursuing them about two hundred yards and rising a little hill, I discovered they were met by another party, and had halted and were reloading their guns. (This was a small party from Jerusalem who knew the Negroes were in the field and had just tied their horses to await their return to the road knowing that Mr. Parker and family were in Jerusalem, but knew nothing of the party that had gone in with Captain Peete. On hearing the firing they immediately rushed to the spot and arrived just in time to arrest the progress of these barbarous villains and save the lives of their friends and fellow citizens.)

Thinking that those who retreated first, and the party who fired on us at fifty or sixty yards distant, had all only fallen back to meet others with ammunition. As I saw them reloading their guns, and more coming up than I saw at first, and several of my bravest men being wounded, the others became panic-struck and scattered over the field; the white men pursued and fired on us several times. Hark had his horse shot under him, and I caught another for him as it was running by me; five or six of my men were wounded, but none left on the field. Finding myself defeated here I instantly determined to go through a private way and cross the Nottoway River at the Cypress Bridge, three miles below Jerusalem, and attack that place in the rear, as I expected they would look for me on the other road, and I had a great desire to get there to procure arms and ammunition. After going a short distance in this private way, accompanied by about twenty men, I overtook two or three who told me the other men were dispersed in every direction. After trying in vain to collect a sufficient force to proceed to Jerusalem, I determined to return, as I was sure they would make back to their old neighborhood, where they would rejoin me, make new recruits, and come down again. On my way back, I called at Mrs. Thomas's, Mrs. Spencer's, and several other places; the white families having fled, we found no more victims to gratify our thirst for blood. We stopped at Maj. Ridley's quarter for the night, and being joined by four of his men, with the recruits made since my defeat, we mustered now about forty strong.

After placing out sentinels, I laid down to sleep, but was quickly roused by a great racket. Starting up, I found some mounted and others in great confusion. One of the sentinels having given the alarm that we were about to be attacked, I ordered some to ride around and reconnoiter, and on their return the others being more alarmed, not knowing who they were, fled in different ways, so that I was reduced to about twenty again. With this I determined to attempt to recruit, and proceed on to rally in the neighborhood I had left. Dr. Blunt's was the nearest house, which we reached just before day; on riding up the yard, Hark fired a gun. We expected Dr. Blunt and his family were at Maj. Ridley's, as I knew there was a company of men there; the gun was fired to ascertain if any of the family were at home. We were immediately fired on and retreated, leaving several of my men. I do not know what became of them, as I never saw them afterward.

Pursuing our course back and coming in sight of Captain Harris's, where we had been the day before, we discovered a party of white men at the house, on which all deserted me but two (Jacob and Nat). We concealed ourselves in the woods until near night, when I sent them in search of Henry, Sam, Nelson, and Hark, and directed them to rally all they could at the place we had had our dinner the Sunday before, where they would find me, and I accordingly returned there as soon as it was dark and remained until Wednesday evening, when discovering white men riding around the place as though they were looking for someone, and none of my men joining me, I concluded Jacob and Nat had been taken and compelled to betray me.

On this I gave up all hope for the present, and on Thursday night, after having supplied myself with provisions from Mr. Travis's, I scratched a hole under a pile of fence rails in a field, where I concealed myself for six weeks, never leaving my hiding place but for a few minutes in the dead of night to get water, which was very near. Thinking by this time I could venture out, I began to go about in the night and eavesdrop the houses in the neighborhood; pursuing this course for about a fortnight and gathering little or no intelligence, afraid of speaking to any human being, and returning every morning to my cave before the dawn of day. I know not how long I might have led this life, if accident had not betrayed me. A dog in the neighborhood, passing by my hiding place one night while I was out, was attracted by some meat I had in my cave, and crawled in and stole it, and was coming out just as I returned. A few nights after, two Negroes having started to go hunting with the same dog, and passed that way, the dog came again to the place, and having just gone out to walk about, discovered me and barked, on which thinking myself discovered, I spoke to them to beg concealment. On making myself known, they fled from me. Knowing then they would betray me, I immediately left my hiding place and was pursued almost incessantly until I was taken a fortnight afterward by Mr. Benjamin Phipps, in a little hole I had dug out with my sword, for the purpose of concealment, under the top of a fallen tree. On Mr. Phipps discovering the place of my concealment, he cocked his gun and aimed at me. I requested him not to shoot and I would give up, upon which he demanded my sword. I delivered it to him, and he brought me to prison. During the time I was pursued, I had many hairsbreadth escapes, which your time will not permit you to relate. I am here loaded with chains, and willing to suffer the fate that awaits me.

Turner was not captured until October 30, 1831, when Benjamin Phipps discovered his hiding place.

LEFT: *The Slave Deck of the Bark "Wildfire,"* illustration from *Harper's Weekly* (June 2, 1860). Although importing slaves into the United States was made illegal in 1808, the slave trade continued on a small scale until the Civil War.

BELOW: *United States Slave Trade, 1830.* Abolitionists used this engraving to raise awareness of their cause.

BOTTOM LEFT: Broadside announcing the sale of Africans in 1769

CHARLESTOWN, *April* 27, 1769.

TO BE SOLD,

On WEDNESDAY *the Tenth Day of* MAY *next*,

A CHOICE CARGO OF

Two Hundred & Fifty

NEGROES:

ARRIVED in the Ship
COUNTESS of SUSSEX, THOMAS DAVIES,
Mafter, directly from GAMBIA, by

JOHN CHAPMAN, & Co.

⁎⁎⁎ THIS is the Veffel that had the Small-Pox on Board at the Time of her Arrival the 31ft of March laft: Every neceffary Precaution hath fince been taken to cleanfe both Ship and Cargo thoroughly, fo that thofe who may be inclined to purchafe need not be under the leaft Apprehenfion of Danger from Infection.

The NEGROES are allowed to be the likelieft Parcel that have been imported this Seafon.

1769

RIGHT: Notice warning African Americans in Boston. Although fugitives had always been subject to being captured and returned into slavery, the 1850 Fugitive Slave Act gave the federal government the authority to bypass local and state legal processes and institutions. Many former slaves had to flee to Canada, and freeborn blacks could be seized and sent to the South as slaves.

CAUTION!!
COLORED PEOPLE
OF BOSTON, ONE & ALL,

You are hereby respectfully CAUTIONED and advised, to avoid conversing with the

Watchmen and Police Officers of Boston,

For since the recent ORDER OF THE MAYOR & ALDERMEN, they are empowered to act as

KIDNAPPERS
AND
Slave Catchers,

And they have already been actually employed in KIDNAPPING, CATCHING, AND KEEPING SLAVES. Therefore, if you value your LIBERTY, and the *Welfare of the Fugitives* among you, *Shun* them in every possible manner, as so many *HOUNDS* on the track of the most unfortunate of your race.

Keep a Sharp Look Out for KIDNAPPERS, and have TOP EYE open.

APRIL 24, 1851.

LEFT: Former slaves sorting cotton on a southern plantation

BELOW: *A Northern Freeman Enslaved by Northern Hands* (1839), illustration from the *Anti-Slavery Almanac* depicting the 1836 kidnapping in New York of a free black man, who was then sent to the South into slavery

ABOVE: *On to Liberty* (1867) by Theodor Kaufmann

LEFT: Two young runaway slaves, circa 1863

Henry Highland Garnet, circa 1881

After escaping slavery with his entire family as a child, Henry Highland Garnet (1815–1882) became a Presbyterian minister and a controversial advocate of black liberation through noncompliance and violent resistance. His most famous speech, "An Address to the Slaves of the United States of America," was delivered in 1843 at the National Negro Convention in Buffalo, New York.

An Address to the Slaves of the United States of America

Henry Highland Garnet

Brethren and Fellow Citizens: Your brethren of the North, East, and West have been accustomed to meet together in national conventions, to sympathize with each other, and to weep over your unhappy condition. In these meetings we have addressed all classes of the free, but we have never, until this time, sent a word of consolation and advice to you. We have been contented in sitting still and mourning over your sorrows, earnestly hoping that before this day your sacred liberties would have been restored. But, we have hoped in vain. Years have rolled on, and tens of thousands have been borne on streams of blood and tears to the shores of eternity. While you have been oppressed, we have also been partakers with you; nor can we be free while you are enslaved. We, therefore, write to you as being bound with you.

Many of you are bound to us, not only by the ties of a common humanity, but we are connected by the more tender relations of parents, wives, husbands, and sisters, and friends. As such we most affectionately address you.

Slavery has fixed a deep gulf between you and us, and while it shuts out from you the relief and consolation which your friends would willingly render, it afflicts and persecutes you with a fierceness which we might not expect to see in the fiends of hell. But still the Almighty Father of mercies has left to us a glimmering ray of hope, which shines out like a lone star in a cloudy sky. Mankind are becoming wiser and better, the oppressor's power is fading, and you, every day, are becoming better informed and more numerous. Your grievances, brethren, are many. We shall not attempt, in this short address, to present to the world all the dark catalog of the nation's sins, which have been committed upon an innocent people. Nor is it indeed necessary, for you feel them from day to day, and all the civilized world looks upon them with amazement.

Two hundred and twenty-seven years ago the first of our injured race were brought to the shores of America. They came not with glad spirits to select their homes in the New World. They came not with their own consent, to find an unmolested enjoyment of the blessings of this fruitful soil. The first dealings they had with men calling themselves Christians exhibited to them the worst features of corrupt and sordid hearts, and convinced them that no cruelty is too great, no villainy and no robbery too abhorrent for even enlightened men to perform, when influenced by avarice and lust. Neither did they come flying upon the wings of liberty to a land of freedom. But they came with broken hearts, from their beloved native land, and were doomed to unrequited toil and deep degradation. Nor did the evil of their bondage end at their emancipation by death. Succeeding generations inherited their chains, and millions have come from eternity into time, and have returned again to the world of spirits, cursed and ruined by American slavery.

The propagators of the system, or their immediate successors, very soon discovered its growing evil and its tremendous wickedness, and secret promises were made to destroy it. The gross inconsistency of a people holding slaves, who had themselves "ferried o'er the wave" for freedom's sake, was too apparent to be entirely overlooked. The voice of freedom cried, "Emancipate your slaves." Humanity supplicated with tears for the deliverance of the children of Africa. Wisdom urged her solemn plea. The bleeding captive pled his innocence, and pointed to Christianity who stood weeping at the cross. Jehovah frowned upon the nefarious institution, and thunderbolts, red with vengeance, struggled to leap forth to blast the guilty wretches who maintained it. But all was vain. Slavery had stretched its dark wings of death over the land, the Church stood silently by, the priests prophesied falsely, and the people loved to have it so. Its throne is established, and now it reigns triumphant.

Nearly three million of your fellow citizens are prohibited by law and public opinion (which in this country is stronger than law) from reading the Book of Life.* Your intellect has been destroyed as much as possible, and every ray of light they have attempted to shut out from your minds. The oppressors themselves have become involved in the ruin. They have become weak, sensual, and rapacious—they have cursed you—they have cursed themselves—they have cursed the earth which they have trod.

* [The Bible—Eds.]

The colonies threw the blame upon England. They said that the mother country entailed the evil upon them, and they would rid themselves of it if they could. The world thought they were sincere, and the philanthropic pitied them. But time soon tested their sincerity. In a few years the colonists grew strong, and severed themselves from the British government. Their independence was declared, and they took their station among the sovereign powers of the earth. The declaration was a glorious document. Sages admired it, and the patriotic of every nation reverenced the God-like sentiments which it contained. When the power of government returned to their hands, did they emancipate the slaves? No; they rather added new links to our chains. Were they ignorant of the principles of liberty? Certainly they were not. The sentiments of their revolutionary orators fell in burning eloquence upon their hearts, and with one voice they cried, LIBERTY OR DEATH. Oh, what a sentence was that! It ran from soul to soul like electric fire, and nerved the arms of thousands to fight in the holy cause of freedom. Among the diversity of opinions that are entertained in regard to physical resistance, there are but a few found to gainsay the stern declaration. We are among those who do not.

SLAVERY! How much misery is comprehended in that single word. What mind is there that does not shrink from its direful effects? Unless the image of God be obliterated from the soul, all men cherish the love of liberty. The nice discerning political economist does not regard the sacred right more than the untutored African who roams in the wilds of Congo. Nor has the one more right to the full enjoyment of his freedom than the other. In every man's mind the good seeds of liberty are planted, and he who brings his fellow down so low, as to make him contented with a condition of slavery, commits the highest crime against God and man. Brethren, your oppresors aim to do this. They endeavor to make you as much like brutes as possible. When they have blinded the eyes of your mind—when they have embittered the sweet waters of life—when they have shut out the light which shines from the word of God—then, and not till then, has American slavery done its perfect work.

TO SUCH DEGRADATION IT IS SINFUL IN THE EXTREME FOR YOU TO MAKE VOLUNTARY SUBMISSION. The divine commandments you are in duty bound to reverence and obey. If you do not obey them, you will surely meet with the displeasure of the Almighty. He requires you to love Him supremely and your neighbor as yourself, to keep the Sabbath day holy, to search the scriptures and bring up your children with respect for his laws, and to worship no other God but him. But slavery sets all these at nought, and hurls defiance in the face of Jehovah. The forlorn condition in which you are placed does not destroy your obligation to God. You are not certain of heaven, because you allow yourselves to remain in a state of slavery, where you cannot obey the commandments of the sovereign of the universe. If the ignorance of slavery is a passport to heaven, then it is a blessing, and no curse, and you should rather desire its perpetuity than its abolition. God will not receive slavery, nor ignorance, nor any other state of mind, for love and obedience to him. Your condition does not absolve you from your moral obligation. The diabolical injustice by which your liberties are cloven down, NEITHER GOD NOR ANGELS, OR JUST MEN, COMMAND YOU TO SUFFER FOR A SINGLE MOMENT. THEREFORE IT IS YOUR SOLEMN AND IMPERATIVE DUTY TO USE EVERY MEANS—MORAL, INTELLECTUAL, AND PHYSICAL—THAT PROMISES SUCCESS. If a band of heathen men should attempt to enslave a race of Christians, and to place their children under the influence of some false religion, surely heaven would frown upon the men who would not resist such aggression, even to death. If, on the other hand, a band of Christians should attempt to enslave a race of heathen men, and to entail slavery upon them, and to keep them in heathenism in the mids't of Christianity, the God of heaven would smile upon every effort which the injured might make to disenthral themselves.

Brethren, it is as wrong for your lordly oppressors to keep you in slavery as it was for the man-thief to steal our ancestors from the coast of Africa. You should therefore now use the same manner of resistance as would have been just in our ancestors when the bloody footprints of the first remorseless soul-thief was placed upon the shores of our fatherland. The humblest peasant is as free in the sight of God as the proudest monarch that ever swayed a scepter. Liberty is a spirit sent out from God, and like its great author, is no respecter of persons.

Brethren, the time has come when you must act for yourselves. It is an old and true saying that "if hereditary bondmen would be free, they must themselves strike the blow." You can plead your own cause, and do the work of emancipation better than any others. The nations of the Old World are moving in the great cause of universal freedom, and some of them at least will, ere long, do you justice. The combined powers of Europe have placed their broad seal of disapprobation upon the African slave trade. But in the slaveholding parts of the United States the trade is as brisk as ever. They buy and sell you as though you were brute beasts. The North has done much—her opinion of slavery in the abstract is known. But in regard to the South, we adopt the opinion of the *New York Evangelist*—"We have advanced so far, that the cause apparently waits for a more effectual door to be thrown open than has been yet." We are about to point you to that more effectual door. Look around you, and behold the bosoms of your loving wives heaving with untold agonies! Hear the cries of your poor children! Remember the stripes your fathers bore. Think of the torture and disgrace of your noble mothers. Think of your wretched sisters, loving virtue and purity, as they are driven into concubinage and are exposed to the unbridled lusts of incarnate devils. Think of the undying glory that hangs around the ancient name of Africa—and forget not that you are native-born American citizens, and as such you are justly entitled to all the rights that are granted to the freest. Think how many tears you have poured out upon the soil which you have cultivated with unrequited toil and enriched with your blood; and then go to your lordly enslavers and tell them plainly, that you *are determined to be free.* Appeal to their sense of justice, and tell them that they have no more right to oppress you than you have to enslave them. Entreat them to remove the grievous burdens which they have imposed upon you, and to remunerate you for your labor. Promise them renewed diligence in the cultivation of the soil, if they will render to you an equivalent for your services. Point them to the increase of happiness and prosperity in the British West Indies since the Act of Emancipation. Tell them in language which they cannot misunderstand of the exceeding sinfulness of slavery, and of a future judgment, and of the righteous retributions of an indignant God. Inform them that all you desire is FREEDOM, and that nothing else will suffice. Do this, and forever after cease to toil for the heartless tyrants who give you no other reward but stripes and abuse. If they then commence work of death, they, and not you, will be responsible for the consequences. You had far better all die—*die immediately*—than live slaves, and entail your wretchedness upon your posterity. If you would be free in this generation, here is your only hope. However much you and all of us may desire it, there is not much hope of redemption without the shedding of blood. If you must bleed, let it all come at once—rather *die freemen than live to be the slaves.* It is impossible, like the children of Israel, to make a grand exodus from the land of bondage. The pharaohs are on both sides of the blood-red waters! You cannot move *en masse* to the dominions of the British queen—nor can you pass through Florida and overrun Texas; and at last find peace in Mexico. The propagators of American slavery are spending their blood and treasure that they may plant the black flag in the heart of Mexico and riot in the halls of the Montezumas. In the language of the Reverend Robert Hall, when addressing the volunteers of Bristol, who were rushing forth to repel the invasion of Napoleon, who threatened to lay waste the fair homes of England, "Religion is too much interested in your behalf not to shed over you her most gracious influences."

You will not be compelled to spend much time in order to become inured to hardships. From the first movement that you breathed the air of heaven, you have been accustomed to nothing else but hardships. The heroes of the American Revolution were never put upon harder fare than a peck of corn and a few herrings per week. You have not become enervated by the luxuries of life. Your sternest energies have been beaten out upon the anvil of severe trial. Slavery has done this to make you subservient to its own purposes; but it has done more than this, it has prepared you for any emergency. If you receive good treatment, it is what you can hardly expect, If you meet with pain, sorrow, and even death, these are the common lot of the slaves.

Fellow men! Patient sufferers! Behold your dearest rights crushed to the earth! See your sons murdered, and your wives, mothers, and sisters doomed to prostitution. In the name of the merciful God, and by all that life is worth, let it no longer be a debatable question, whether it is better to choose *liberty* or *death*.

In 1822, Denmark Veazie, of South Carolina, formed a plan for the liberation of his fellow men. In the whole history of human efforts to overthrow slavery, a more complicated and tremendous plan was never formed. He was betrayed by the treachery of his own people, and died a martyr to freedom. Many a brave hero fell, but history, faithful to her high trust, will transcribe his name on the same monument with Moses, Hampden, Tell, Bruce and Wallace, Toussaint L'Ouverture, Lafayette, and Washington. That tremendous movement shook the whole empire of slavery. The guilty soul-thieves were overwhelmed with fear. It is a matter of fact that at this time, and in consequence of the threatened revolution, the slave states talked strongly of emancipation. But they blew but one blast of the trumpet of freedom, and then laid it aside. As these men became quiet, the slaveholders ceased to talk about emancipation: and now behold your condition today! Angels sigh over it, and humanity has long since exhausted her tears in weeping on your account!

The patriotic Nathaniel Turner followed Denmark Veazie. He was goaded to desperation by wrong and injustice. By despotism, his name has been recorded on the list of infamy, and future generations will remember him among the noble and brave.

Next arose the immortal Joseph Cinque, the hero of the *Amistad*. He was a native African, and by the help of God he emancipated a whole shipload of his fellow men on the high seas. And he now sings of liberty on the sunny hills of Africa and beneath his native palm trees, where he hears the lion roar and feels himself as free as the king of the forest.

Next arose Madison Washington, that bright star of freedom, and took his station in the constellation of true heroism. He was a slave onboard the brig *Creole*, of Richmond, bound to New Orleans, that great slave mart, with a hundred and four others. Nineteen struck for liberty or death. But one life was taken, and the whole were emancipated, and the vessel was carried into Nassau, New Providence.

Noble men! Those who have fallen in freedom's conflict, their memories will be cherished by the true-hearted and the God-fearing in all future generations; those who are living, their names are surrounded by a halo of glory.

Brethren, arise, arise! Strike for your lives and liberties. Now is the day and the hour. Let every slave throughout the land do this, and the days of slavery are numbered. You cannot be more oppressed than you have been—you cannot suffer greater cruelties than you have already. *Rather die as freemen than live to be slaves.* Remember that you are FOUR MILLION!

It is in your power so to torment the God-cursed slaveholders that they will be glad to let you go free. If the scale was turned, and black men were the masters and white men the slaves, every destructive agent and element would be employed to lay the oppressor low. Danger and death would hang over their heads day and night. Yes, the tyrants would meet with plagues more terrible than those of Pharaoh. But you are a patient people. You act as though you were made for the special use of these devils. You act as though your daughters were born to pamper the lusts of your masters and overseers. And worse than all, you tamely submit while your lords tear your wives from your embraces and defile them before your eyes. In the name of God, we ask, are you men? Where is the blood of your fathers? Has it all run out of your veins? Awake, awake; millions of voices are calling you! Your dead fathers speak to you from their graves. Heaven, as with a voice of thunder, calls on you to arise from the dust.

Let your motto be resistance! *Resistance!* RESISTANCE! No oppressed people have ever secured their liberty without resistance. What kind of resistance you had better make you must decide by the circumstances that surround you, and according to the suggestion of expediency. Brethren, adieu! Trust in the living God. Labor for the peace of the human race, and remember that you are FOUR MILLION!

An American Slave Market (1852) by Taylor

Born free, Solomon Northrup (1808–1862?) was kidnapped into slavery from Washington, D.C., in 1841. Twelve years later, he regained his freedom. This selection is from his narrative about his experience, *Twelve Years a Slave* (1853).

A Slave Auction

Solomon Northrup

The very amiable, pious-hearted Mr. Theophilus Freeman, a partner or consignee of James H. Burch, and keeper of the slave pen in New Orleans, was out among his animals early in the morning. With an occasional kick of the older men and women, and many a sharp crack of the whip about the ears of the younger slaves, it was not long before they were all astir and wide awake. Mr. Theophilus Freeman bustled about in a very industrious manner, getting his property ready for the salesroom, intending, no doubt, to do that day a rousing business.

In the first place we were required to wash thoroughly, and those with beards to shave. We were then furnished with a new suit each, cheap, but clean. The men had hat, coat, shirt, pants, and shoes; the women frocks of calico, and handkerchief to bind about their heads. We were now conducted into a large room in the front part of the building to which the yard was attached, in order to be properly trained, before the admission of customers. The men were arranged on one side of the room, the women at the other. The tallest was placed at the head of the row, then the next tallest, and so on in the order of their respective heights. Emily was at the foot of the line of women. Freeman charged us to remember our places and exhorted us to appear smart and lively— sometimes threatening, and again, holding out various inducements. During the day he exercised us in the art of "looking smart," and of moving to our places with exact precision.

After being fed, in the afternoon, we were again paraded and made to dance. Bob, a colored boy, who had some time belonged to Freeman, played on the violin. Standing near him, I made bold to inquire if he could play the "Virginia Reel." He answered he could not, and asked me if I could play. Replying in the affirmative, he handed me the violin. I struck up a tune, and finished it. Freeman ordered me to continue playing, and seemed well pleased, telling Bob that I far excelled him—a remark that seemed to grieve my musical companion very much.

Next day many customers called to examine Freeman's "new lot." The latter gentleman was very loquacious, dwelling at much length upon our personal good points and qualities. He would make us hold up our heads, walk briskly back and forth, while customers would feel of our hands and arms and bodies, turn us about, ask us what we could do, make us open our mouths and show our teeth, precisely as a jockey examines a horse which he is about to barter for or purchase. Sometimes a man or woman was taken back to the small house in the yard, stripped, and inspected more minutely. Scars upon a slave's back were considered evidence of a rebellious or unruly spirit, and hurt his sale.

One old gentleman, who said he wanted a coachman, appeared to take a fancy to me. From his conversation with Burch, I learned he was a resident in the city. I very much desired that he would buy me, because I conceived it would not be difficult to make my escape from New Orleans on some northern vessel. Freeman asked him fifteen hundred dollars for me. The old gentleman insisted it was too much, as times were very hard. Freeman, however, declared that I was sound and healthy, of good constitution, and intelligent. He made it a point to enlarge upon my musical attainments. The old gentleman argued quite adroitly that there was nothing extraordinary about the nigger, and finally, to my regret, went out, saying he would call again. During the day, however, a number of sales were made. David and Caroline were purchased together by a Natchez planter. They left us, grinning broadly, and in the most happy state of mind, caused by the fact of their not being separated. Lethe was sold to a planter of Baton Rouge, her eyes flashing with anger as she was led away.

The same man also purchased Randall. The little fellow was made to jump, and run across the floor, and perform many other feats exhibiting his activity and condition. All the time the trade was going on, Eliza was crying aloud and wringing her hands. She besought the man not to buy him, unless he also bought herself and Emily. She promised, in that case, to be the most faithful slave that ever lived. The man answered that he could not afford it, and then Eliza burst into a paroxysm of grief, weeping plaintively. Freeman turned round to her, savagely, with his whip in his uplifted hand, ordering her to stop her noise, or he would flog her. He would not have such work—such sniveling; and unless she ceased that minute, he would take her to the yard and give her a hundred lashes. Yes, he would take the nonsense out of her pretty quick—if he didn't, might he be d——d. Eliza shrunk before him, and tried to wipe away her tears, but it was all in vain. She wanted to be with her children, she said, the little time she had to live. All the frowns and threats of Freeman, could not wholly silence the afflicted mother. She kept on begging and beseeching them, most piteously, not to separate the three. Over and over again she told them how she loved her boy. A great many times she repeated her former promises—how very faithful and obedient she would be; how hard she would labor day and night, to the last moment of her life, if he would only buy them all together. But it was of no avail; the man could not afford it. The bargain was agreed upon, and Randall must go alone. Then Eliza ran to him; embraced him passionately; kissed him again and again; told him to remember her—all the while her tears falling in the boy's face like rain.

Freeman damned her, calling her a blubbering, bawling wench, and ordered her to go to her place, and behave herself, and be somebody. He swore he wouldn't stand such stuff but a little longer. He would soon give her something to cry about, if she was not mighty careful, and *that* she might depend upon.

The planter from Baton Rouge, with his new purchases, was ready to depart.

"Don't cry, mama. I will be a good boy. Don't cry," said Randall, looking back, as they passed out of the door.

What has become of the lad, God knows. It was a mournful scene indeed. I would have cried myself if I had dared.

This selection is taken from William S. McFeely's *Frederick Douglass* (1991), the most comprehensive biography of Douglass. Here McFeely addresses the circumstances of the writing of the *Narrative*, as well as the choices Douglass made about what to omit from the book.

The Narrative as Literature

William S. McFeely

He was, in fact, determined to be something far beyond a curiosity when in 1844 he began to write a story of his life that would make the world pay him true attention. His book, he and his friends felt sure, not only would reach readers who had not heard him, but would also reinforce the picture in the mind's eye, the sonorous sound still in the ear, of those who had. Wendell Phillips, in particular, urged him to write his story, and in the spring of 1845 was telling his audiences to be on the lookout for it. The *Narrative of the Life of Frederick Douglass* would be a powerful antislavery tract, but it would also be far more than that.

In his writing, Douglass outran being a runaway. Never satisfied with the degree to which a nineteenth-century white world took the ex-slave seriously as an intellectual, he would have been profoundly gratified by the attention paid his work in the twentieth century. Read now only secondarily for what they tell us about slavery, his *Narrative* (1845) and *My Bondage and My Freedom* (1855) have earned the regard of critics, such as William L. Andrews, who see them as two in the series of great "I" narratives of that most remarkable of all decades of American letters. The *Narrative* carries none of the poetry of Whitman's first edition of *Leaves of Grass* (1855), but it too is a song of myself. There is not the epic tragedy of Melville's *Moby-Dick* (1851), and yet it is a story—not wholly unlike Ishmael's—of survival in a world at sea with evil. On the other hand, with its message of growing self-confidence, of self-reliance, the *Narrative* is kin to Emerson's essays. But perhaps Douglass's telling of his odyssey is closest cousin to Thoreau's account of his altogether safe escape to Walden Pond. That quietly contained, subversive tale has reverberated ever since its telling with a message of radical repudiation of corrupt society. Thoreau heard a Wendell Phillips lecture describing Douglass's exodus—and reporting that a written account was on its way—in the spring of 1845 as he was planning his sojourn outside Concord. Robert D. Richardson Jr., who wrote Thoreau's intellectual biography, has said that it is not "an accident that the earliest stages of Thoreau's move to Walden coincide with . . . the publication of Douglass's narrative of how he gained his freedom. *Walden* is about self-emancipation."

In all three of his autobiographies, Douglass tantalizes us with the many things he leaves out; not the least of these is discussion of why and how he wrote them. His correspondence is equally void of references to what must have been a compelling exercise for him. We know that Phillips and others in the Anti-Slavery Society urged him to put his story into print, but whom did he talk to about the project, who helped, who was its editor? His later quarrels with his British publisher make it clear that he cared not only about the content—he resisted any censoring of material thought to be offensive to Christians—but also about the appearance of the front matter and the cover. Such concerns must have been with Douglass even at the time of the first printing of the first book.

But perhaps not. To a remarkable degree *Narrative of the Life of Frederick Douglass* does seem to have simply sprung from a man who had been telling the same story in much the same language from the antislavery platform for four years. And once he had created, with his voice and then his pencil, the Frederick Douglass of the *Narrative,* the author never altered either the character or the plot significantly. This, more than the fact that speaking came easier than writing for Douglass, explains why he wrote no books other than the autobiographies. He had but one character to craft, one story to tell. The two later books, *My Bondage and My Freedom* and *Life and Times of Frederick Douglass,* reveal important shifts in approach and detail, but the Frederick Douglass of the *Narrative* remains inviolate.

The *Narrative* is short and direct, from the "I was born" of its first line to its closing account of the Nantucket speech, describing how Douglass "felt strongly moved to speak" and was urged to do so as well: "It was a severe cross, and I took it up reluctantly. The truth was, I felt myself a slave, and the idea of speaking to white people weighed me down. I spoke but a few moments, when I felt a degree of freedom." The person we come to know in these brief pages is unforgettable. From the *Narrative* and the many other accounts of runaways published in Douglass's day, right down to Toni Morrison's *Beloved* in ours, there has been no escape from the slave in American letters. And for the fifty years following publication of the *Narrative* in 1845, there was no escape for the author from the runaway he had created.

It is easy when reading the *Narrative* to misjudge the reason for the author's many omissions—the nature of his relationships with his brothers and sisters, for example. His focused concentration on himself does invite the charge of insensitivity to others. But there were other, deeper reasons for such voids. We get a hint of them when he tells of slaves on a Wye House farm singing "most exultingly" when "leaving home: . . . they would sing, as a chorus, to words which to many would seem unmeaning jargon, but which, nevertheless, were full of meaning to themselves." There were some sounds of slavery that Douglass could not render in words that his readers would hear, private torments and horrors too deep in the well to be drawn up.

The book was published by the "Anti-Slavery Office" in Boston in June 1845 and priced at fifty cents. The *Liberator* had announced its publication in May, and Phillips and his allies in the literary world saw to it that reviews appeared promptly. By fall, 4,500 copies had been sold in the United States; soon there were three European editions, and within five years 30,000 copies were in the hands of readers. The inevitable charge appeared that a slave boy could not have written the book—Lydia Maria Child (also falsely credited with having written Harriet Jacobs's *Incidents in the Life of a Slave Girl*) was one of many suspected of having been the ghostwriter. But anyone who had heard Douglass—and by 1845 thousands of people had—knew that the language of the *Narrative* was the same as that of the man who so passionately told his tale from the platform.

Douglass's desk at Cedar Hill, his home in Washington, D.C.

Elizabeth Cady Stanton (1815–1902) was a major force in the women's rights movement in the United States for much of the nineteenth century. She was also involved in the antislavery movement, meeting Frederick Douglass in the 1840s. Stanton wrote this diary entry the day after Douglass died.

Frederick Douglass Is Dead!

Elizabeth Cady Stanton

New York, February 21 [1895]—Taking up the papers today, the first word that caught my eye thrilled my very soul. Frederick Douglass is dead! What memories of the long years since he and I first met chased each other, thick and fast, through my mind and held me spellbound. A graduate from the "Southern Institution," he was well fitted to stand before a Boston audience and, with his burning eloquence, portray his sufferings in the land of bondage. He stood there like an African prince, majestic in his wrath, as with wit, satire, and indignation he graphically described the bitterness of slavery and the humiliation of subjection to those who, in all human virtues and powers, were inferior to himself. Thus it was that I first saw Frederick Douglass, and wondered that any mortal man should have ever tried to subjugate a being with such talents, intensified with the love of liberty. Around him sat the great antislavery orators of the day, earnestly watching the effect of his eloquence on that immense audience, that laughed and wept by turns, completely carried away by the wondrous gifts of his pathos and humor. On this occasion, all the other speakers seemed tame after Frederick Douglass. In imitation of the Methodist preachers of the South, he used to deliver a sermon from the text, "Servants, obey your masters," which some of our literary critics pronounced the finest piece of satire in the English language. The last time I visited his home at Anacostia, near Washington, I asked him if he had the written text of that sermon. He answered, "No, not even notes of it." "Could you give it again?" I asked. "No," he replied; "or at least I could not bring back the old feelings even if I tried, the blessing of liberty I have so long enjoyed having almost obliterated the painful memories of my sad early days."

Douglass, Frederick

NARRATIVE

OF THE

LIFE

OF

FREDERICK DOUGLASS,

AN

AMERICAN SLAVE,

WRITTEN BY HIMSELF.

BOSTON:
PUBLISHED AT THE ANTI-SLAVERY OFFICE,
No. 25 CORNHILL.
1849

Frederick Douglass

THE FUGITIVE'S SONG,

WORDS

FREDERICK DOUGLASS
A Graduate from the
"PECULIAR INSTITUTION"

HIS BROTHERS IN BONDS.

FUGITIVES FROM SLAVERY

FREE STATES & CANADAS.

JESSE HUTCHINSON JUNR

BOSTON Published by HENRY PRENTISS 33 Court St

ABOVE: Title page and engraved portrait of Douglass from the first edition of the *Narrative*

LEFT: Sheet music for "The Fugitive's Song," which is dedicated to Douglass

LEFT: Douglass with grandson Joseph Douglass playing a violin

BELOW: Douglass in a photograph taken around 1879

BACKGROUND: Cedar Hill, Douglass's home in Washington, D.C., where he lived from 1878 until his death in 1895

Marqu (1840–1841) by William Townsend. This drawing and those on pages 124 and 125 show Africans who were aboard the *Amistad,* a Spanish slave ship bound for Cuba. On July 2, 1839, the Africans revolted, but the ship was seized by the U.S. Navy off the coast of Long Island, New York. The Africans who survived the mutiny were imprisoned until, in 1841, the Supreme Court ruled that they were free to return home.

Called "the poet laureate of the Negro race" by Booker T. Washington, Paul Laurence Dunbar (1872–1906), the son of former slaves, achieved enormous popular success during his short lifetime. Dunbar has since been praised as well as criticized for his treatment of black themes and his use of black dialect in his poetry.

Poems

Paul Laurence Dunbar

We Wear the Mask

We wear the mask that grins and lies,
It hides our checks and shades our eyes,—
This debt we pay to human guile;
With torn and bleeding hearts we smile,
And mouth with myriad subtleties.

Why should the world be overwise,
In counting all our tears and sighs?
Nay, let them only see us, while
    We wear the mask.

We smile, but, O great Christ, our cries
To thee from tortured souls arise.
We sing, but oh the clay is vile
Beneath our feet, and long the mile;
But let the world dream otherwise,
    We wear the mask!

Sympathy

I know what the caged bird feels, alas!
    When the sun is bright on the upland slopes;
When the wind stirs soft through the springing grass,
And the river flows like a stream of glass;
    When the first bird sings and the first bud opes,
And the faint perfume from its chalice steals—
I know what the caged bird feels!

I know why the caged bird beats his wing
    Till its blood is red on the cruel bars;
For he must fly back to his perch and cling
When he fain would be on the bough a-swing;
    And a pain still throbs in the old, old scars
And they pulse again with a keener sting—
I know why he beats his wing!

I know why the caged bird sings, ah me,
    When his wing is bruised and his bosom sore,—
When he beats his bars and he would be free;
It is not a carol of joy or glee,
    But a prayer that he sends from his heart's deep core,
But a plea, that upward to Heaven he flings—
I know why the caged bird sings!

Fuli (1840–1841)
by William Townsend

Douglass

Ah, Douglass, we have fall'n on evil days,
    Such days as thou, not even thou didst know,
    When thee, the eyes of that harsh long ago
Saw, salient, at the cross of devious ways,
And all the country heard thee with amaze.
    Not ended then, the passionate ebb and flow,
    The awful tide that battled to and fro;
We ride amid a tempest of dispraise.

Now, when the waves of swift dissension swarm,
    And Honor, the strong pilot, lieth stark,
Oh, for thy voice high-sounding o'er the storm,
    For thy strong arm to guide the shivering bark,
The blast-defying power of thy form,
    To give us comfort through the lonely dark.

Little Kale (1840–1841)
by William Townsend

125

Harriet Hemmings, Slave Daughter of Thomas Jefferson
(Tragic Mulatto Series, 1999) by Lezley Saar

The primary author of the Declaration of Independence, Thomas Jefferson (1743–1826) was also a slaveholder. This selection is taken from Jefferson's book, *Notes on the State of Virginia* (1784–1785), compiled while he was the governor of Virginia, in response to a request for information about the state.

On Slavery

Thomas Jefferson

There must doubtless be an unhappy influence on the manners of our people produced by the existence of slavery among us. The whole commerce between master and slave is a perpetual exercise of the most boisterous passions, the most unremitting despotism on the one part, and degrading submissions on the other. Our children see this and learn to imitate it, for man is an imitative animal. This quality is the germ of all education in him. From his cradle to his grave he is learning to do what he sees others do. If a parent could find no motive either in his philanthropy or his self-love for restraining the intemperance of passion toward his slave, it should always be a sufficient one that his child is present. But generally it is not sufficient. The parent storms, the child looks on, catches the lineaments of wrath, puts on the same airs in the circle of smaller slaves, gives a loose to the worst of passions, and thus nursed, educated, and daily exercised in tyranny, cannot but be stamped by it with odious peculiarities. The man must be a prodigy who can retain his manners and morals undepraved by such circumstances. And with what execration should the statesman be loaded who, permitting one-half of the citizens thus to trample on the rights of the others, transforms those into despots, and these into enemies, destroys the morals of the one part, and the *amor patriae** of the other. For if a slave can have a country in this world, it must be any other in preference to that in which he is born to live and labor for another; in which he must lock up the faculties of his nature, contribute as far as depends on his individual endeavors to the evanish-

* [Love of one's country.]

ment of the human race, or entail his own miserable condition on the endless generations proceeding from him. With the morals of the people, their industry also is destroyed. For in a warm climate, no man will labor for himself who can make another labor for him. This is so true that, of the proprietors of slaves, a very small proportion indeed are ever seen to labor. And can the liberties of a nation be thought secure when we have removed their only firm basis, a conviction in the minds of the people that these liberties are of the gift of God? That they are not to be violated but with his wrath? Indeed, I tremble for my country when I reflect that God is just; that his justice cannot sleep forever; that considering numbers, nature, and natural means only, a revolution of the wheel of fortune, an exchange of situation, is among possible events; that it may become probable by supernatural interference! The Almighty has no attribute which can take side with us in such a contest. But it is impossible to be temperate and to pursue this subject through the various considerations of policy, of morals, of history natural and civil. We must be contented to hope they will force their way into everyone's mind. I think a change already perceptible, since the origin of the present revolution. The spirit of the master is abating, that of the slave rising from the dust, his condition mollifying, the way, I hope, preparing, under the auspices of heaven, for a total emancipation, and that this is disposed, in the order of events, to be with the consent of the masters, rather than by their extirpation.

A major figure among the mid-nineteenth-century American writers and
philosophers known as the transcendentalists, Henry David Thoreau
(1817–1862) is best known for *Walden* (1854), his account of the years he spent
secluded at Walden Pond near Concord, Massachusetts. Thoreau wrote "Civil
Disobedience" (1849), the essay from which this selection is taken, after
he was jailed for refusing to pay his poll tax.

Civil Disobedience

(SELECTION)

Henry David Thoreau

I do not hesitate to say that those who call themselves abolitionists should at
once effectually withdraw their support, both in person and property, from the
government of Massachusetts, and not wait till they constitute a majority of one
before they suffer the right to prevail through them. I think that it is enough if
they have God on their side, without waiting for that other one. Moreover, any
man more right than his neighbors constitutes a majority of one already.

I meet this American government, or its representative, the state government, directly, and face to face, once a year—no more—in the person of its tax-
gatherer. This is the only mode in which a man situated as I am necessarily
meets it, and it then says distinctly, Recognize me; and the simplest, most effectual, and, in the present posture of affairs, the indispensablest mode of treating
with it on this head, of expressing your little satisfaction with and love for it, is
to deny it then. My civil neighbor, the tax-gatherer, is the very man I have to
deal with—for it is, after all, with men and not with parchment that I quarrel—
and he has voluntarily chosen to be an agent of the government. How shall he
ever know well what he is and does as an officer of the government, or as a man,
until he is obliged to consider whether he shall treat me, his neighbor, for whom
he has respect, as a neighbor and well-disposed man, or as a maniac and
disturber of the peace, and see if he can get over this obstruction to his neighbor-
liness without a ruder and more impetuous thought or speech corresponding
with his action. I know this well, that if one thousand, if one hundred, if ten
men whom I could name—if ten *honest* men only—ay, if *one* HONEST man, in
this State of Massachusetts, *ceasing to hold slaves,* were actually to withdraw

from this copartnership, and be locked up in the county jail therefor, it would be the abolition of slavery in America. For it matters not how small the beginning may seem to be: what is once well done is done forever. But we love better to talk about it: that we say is our mission. Reform keeps many scores of newspapers in its service, but not one man. If my esteemed neighbor, the state's ambassador, who will devote his days to the settlement of the question of human rights in the council chamber, instead of being threatened with the prisons of Carolina were to sit down the prisoner of Massachusetts, that state which is so anxious to foist the sin of slavery upon her sister—though at present she can discover only an act of inhospitality to be the ground of a quarrel with her—the legislature would not wholly waive the subject the following winter.

Under a government which imprisons any unjustly, the true place for a just man is also a prison. The proper place today, the only place which Massachusetts has provided for her freer and less desponding spirits, is in her prisons, to be put out and locked out of the state by her own act, as they have already put themselves out by their principles. It is there that the fugitive slave, and the Mexican prisoner on parole, and the Indian come to plead the wrongs of his race should find them; on that separate but more free and honorable ground, where the state places those who are not *with* her, but *against* her—the only house in a slave state in which a free man can abide with honor. If any think that their influence would be lost there, and their voices no longer afflict the ear of the state, that they would not be as an enemy within its walls, they do not know by how much truth is stronger than error, nor how much more eloquently and effectively he can combat injustice who has experienced a little in his own person. Cast your whole vote, not a strip of paper merely, but your whole influence. A minority is powerless while it conforms to the majority; it is not even a minority then; but it is irresistible when it clogs by its whole weight. If the alternative is to keep all just men in prison, or give up war and slavery, the state will not hesitate which to choose. If a thousand men were not to pay their tax bills this year, that would not be a violent and bloody measure, as it would be to pay them and enable the state to commit violence and shed innocent blood. This is, in fact, the definition of a peaceable revolution, if any such is possible. If the tax-gatherer, or any other public officer, asks me, as one has done, "But what shall I do?" my answer is, "If you really wish to do anything, resign your office." When the subject has refused allegiance, and the officer has resigned his office, then the revolution is accomplished. But even suppose blood should flow. Is there not a sort of blood shed when the conscience is wounded? Through this wound a man's real manhood and immortality flow out, and he bleeds to an everlasting death. I see this blood flowing now.

Perhaps the most radical of the slavery apologists, George Fitzhugh (1806–1881)
defended slavery on the grounds that it was superior to free market capitalism
as an economic system. Fitzhugh also argued that slavery maintained
what he thought was the naturally paternalistic relationship between blacks
and whites, as seen in this selection from his book *Sociology of the South,
or the Failure of Free Society* (1854).

Negro Slavery

George Fitzhugh

It is clear the Athenian democracy would not suit a Negro nation, nor will the
government of mere law suffice for the individual Negro. He is but a grown-up
child and must be governed as a child, not as a lunatic or criminal. The master
occupies toward him the place of parent or guardian. We shall not dwell on this
view, for no one will differ with us who thinks as we do of the Negro's capacity, and we might argue till doomsday, in vain, with those who have a high
opinion of the Negro's moral and intellectual capacity.

Second, the Negro is improvident; will not lay up in summer for the wants
of winter; will not accumulate in youth for the exigencies of age. He would
become an insufferable burden to society. Society has the right to prevent this,
and can only do so by subjecting him to domestic slavery.

In the last place, the Negro race is inferior to the white race, and living in
their midst, they would be far outstripped or outwitted in the chase of free
competition. Gradual but certain extermination would be their fate. We
presume the maddest abolitionist does not think the Negro's providence of
habits and moneymaking capacity at all to compare to those of the whites. This
defect of character would alone justify enslaving him, if he is to remain here.
In Africa or the West Indies, he would become idolatrous, savage, and canni-
bal, or be devoured by savages and cannibals. At the North he would freeze or
starve.

We would remind those who deprecate and sympathize with Negro slavery that his slavery here relieves him from a far more cruel slavery in Africa,
or from idolatry and cannibalism and every brutal vice and crime that can

disgrace humanity; and that it Christianizes, protects, supports, and civilizes him; that it governs him far better than free laborers at the North are governed. There, wife-murder has become a mere holiday pastime; and where so many wives are murdered, almost all must be brutally treated. Nay, more, men who kill their wives or treat them brutally must be ready for all kinds of crime, and the calendar of crime at the North proves the inference to be correct. Negroes never kill their wives. If it be objected that legally they have no wives, then we reply that in an experience of more than forty years, we have never yet heard of a Negro man killing a Negro woman. Our Negroes are not only better off as to physical comfort than free laborers, but their moral condition is better. . . .

Negro slavery would be changed immediately to some form of peonage, serfdom, or villeinage if the Negroes were sufficiently intelligent and provident to manage a farm. No one would have the labor and trouble of management if his Negroes would pay in hires and rents one-half what free tenants pay in rent in Europe. Every Negro in the South would be soon liberated if he would take liberty on the terms that white tenants hold it. The fact that he cannot enjoy liberty on such terms seems conclusive that he is only fit to be a slave.

Would the abolitionists approve of a system of society that set white children free and remitted them at the age of fourteen, males and females, to all the rights, both as to person and property, which belong to adults? Would it be criminal or praiseworthy to do so? Criminal, of course. Now, are the average of Negroes equal in information, in native intelligence, in prudence or providence, to well-informed white children of fourteen? We who have lived with them for forty years think not. The competition of the world would be too much for the children. They would be cheated out of their property and debased in their morals. Yet they would meet everywhere with sympathizing friends of their own color, ready to aid, advise, and assist them. The Negro would be exposed to the same competition and greater temptations, with no greater ability to contend with them, with these additional difficulties. He would be welcome nowhere; meet with thousands of enemies and no friends. If he went North, the white laborers would kick him and cuff him and drive him out of employment; if he went to Africa, the savages would cook him and eat him. If he went to the West Indies, they would not let him in, or if they did, they would soon make of him a savage and idolator.

We have a further question to ask. If it be right and incumbent to subject children to the authority of parents and guardians, and idiots and lunatics to committees, would it not be equally right and incumbent to give the free Negroes masters, until at least they arrive at years of discretion, which very few ever did or will attain? What is the difference between the authority of a parent and of a master? Neither pay wages, and each is entitled to the services of those

subject to him. The father may not sell his child forever, but may hire him out till he is twenty-one. The free Negro's master may also be restrained from selling. Let him stand in *loco parentis,* and call him papa instead of master. Look closely into slavery, and you will see nothing so hideous in it, or if you do, you will find plenty of it at home in its most hideous form.

Abraham Lincoln in 1865

Slavery in the United States was not effectively ended until the passage of the Thirteenth Amendment on December 6, 1865. But the Emancipation Proclamation, issued on January 1, 1863, was a signal that President Abraham Lincoln (1809–1865) had come to believe that the end of slavery was now a goal for which the Civil War was being fought.

Emancipation Proclamation

Abraham Lincoln

Whereas, on the twenty-second day of September, in the year of our Lord one thousand eight hundred and sixty-two, a proclamation was issued by the President of the United States, containing, among other things, the following, to wit:

"That on the first day of January, in the year of our Lord one thousand eight hundred and sixty-three, all persons held as slaves within any state or designated part of a state, the people whereof shall then be in rebellion against the United States, shall be then, thenceforward, and forever, free; and the executive government of the United States, including the military and naval authority thereof, will recognize and maintain the freedom of such persons, and will do no act or acts to repress such persons, or any of them, in any efforts they may make for their actual freedom.

"That the executive will, on the first day of January aforesaid, by proclamation, designate the states and parts of states, if any, in which the people thereof, respectively, shall then be in rebellion against the United States; and the fact that any state, or the people thereof, shall on that day be in good faith represented in the Congress of the United States, by members chosen thereto at elections, wherein a majority of the qualified voters of such states shall have participated, shall, in the absence of strong countervailing testimony, be deemed conclusive evidence that such state, and the people thereof, are not then in rebellion against the United States."

Now, therefore, I, Abraham Lincoln, President of the United States, by virtue of the power in me vested as commander in chief of the army and navy of the United States, in time of actual armed rebellion against the authority and government of the United States, and as a fit and necessary war measure for suppressing said rebellion, do, on this first day of January, in the year of our Lord one thousand eight hundred and sixty-three, and in accordance with my purpose so to do, publicly proclaimed for the full period of one hundred days from the day first above mentioned, order and designate as the states and parts of states wherein the people thereof, respectively, are this day in rebellion against the United States, the following, to wit:

Arkansas, Texas, Louisiana (except the parishes of St. Bernard, Plaquemines, Jefferson, St. John, St. Charles, St. James, Ascension, Assumption, Terre Bonne, Lafourche, St. Mary, St. Martin, and Orleans, including the City of New Orleans), Mississippi, Alabama, Florida, Georgia, South Carolina, North Carolina, and Virginia (except the forty-eight counties designated as West Virginia, and also the counties of Berkeley, Accomac, Northampton, Elizabeth City, York, Princess Ann, and Norfolk, including the cities of Norfolk and Portsmouth), and which excepted parts are for the present left precisely as if this proclamation were not issued.

And by virtue of the power and for the purpose aforesaid, I do order and declare that all persons held as slaves within said designated states and parts of states are, and henceforward shall be, free; and that the executive government of the United States, including the military and naval authorities thereof, will recognize and maintain the freedom of said persons.

And I hereby enjoin upon the people so declared to be free to abstain from all violence, unless in necessary self-defense; and I recommend to them that, all cases when allowed, they labor faithfully for reasonable wages.

And I further declare and make known that such persons, of suitable condition, will be received into the armed service of the United States to garrison forts, positions, stations, and other places, and to man vessels of all sorts in said service.

And upon this act, sincerely believed to be an act of justice, warranted by the Constitution upon military necessity, I invoke the considerate judgment of mankind and the gracious favor of almighty God.

In witness whereof, I have hereunto set my hand and caused the seal of the United States to be affixed.

Done at the city of Washington this first day of January, in the year of our Lord one thousand eight hundred and sixty-three, and of the Independence of the United States of America the eighty-seventh.

Glossary of Literary Terms

allegory A device in which characters and events stand for abstract ideas, principles, or forces, so that the literal situation suggests a deeper symbolic meaning.

alliteration The repetition of identical or nearly identical sounds at the beginning of consecutive or nearby words.

allusion A reference to a person, place, thing, or event, historical or fictional, that suggests a wider frame of reference or greater depth of meaning.

ambiguity A situation expressed in such a way as to allow more than one possible interpretation.

apostrophe A direct address to an inanimate object or an absent or deceased person.

autobiography An account of a person's life written by that person.

climax The point of greatest intensity or complication in a narrative; the turning point in a plot or dramatic action.

connotation The ideas and feelings commonly associated with or suggested by a word.

elegy A formal and sustained lament on the death of a particular person (adj., elegiac).

epiphany A moment of sudden insight or enlightenment that provides a character with new understanding about himself or herself or about a situation.

foreshadowing An indirect suggestion or clues that predict events yet to unfold in a story.

hyperbole A figure of speech that uses exaggeration for emphasis or effect and can also reveal aspects of a character or situation that are not directly stated.

imagery The sensory details in a written work, both literal and figurative, that create vivid impressions and emotional suggestions.

irony The contrast between what is directly relayed (through speech or description) and what is actually meant, or a state of affairs that is the opposite of what is expected.

metaphor A figure of speech that involves an implied or direct comparison between two relatively unlike things.

mood The atmosphere that is created by the author's choice of details and the words used to present them.

motivation The reasoning or emotion that drives a character's actions.

narrative An account or story of actual or fictional events.

paradox An apparent contradiction that is often true under examination.

personification A figure of speech in which human characteristics are assigned to nonhuman things.

point of view The perspective from which a story is told, such as first person, third-person limited, and third-person omniscient.

protagonist The central character around which the story revolves.

rhetoric The art of persuasion; the use of specific devices to achieve the intellectual and emotional effects that will persuade an audience.

setting When and where a story takes place, including aspects of history, geography, season, social circumstances, and atmosphere.

simile A comparison between two unlike things using the word *like* or *as*.

symbol Something that is itself and also stands for something else.

syntax The combination of words into phrases, clauses, and sentences.

theme A central idea in a literary work.

tone The attitude or feeling that pervades a given work, as determined by word choice, style, imagery, connotation, sound, and rhythm.

understatement A figure of speech that uses restraint or indifference to achieve irony or rhetorical effect.

Selected Bibliography

Blassingame, John W., ed. *Slave Testimony: Two Centuries of Letters, Speeches, Interviews, and Autobiographies*. Baton Rouge: Louisiana State University Press, 1977.

Diedrich, Maria. *Love Across the Color Lines: Ottilie Assing and Frederick Douglass*. New York: Hill and Wang, 1999.

Douglass, Frederick. *Life and Times of Frederick Douglass, Written by Himself: His Early Life as a Slave, His Escape from Bondage, and His Complete History to the Present Time*. London: Christian Age Office, 1882. Mineola, NY: Dover Publications, 2003.

——— . *My Bondage and My Freedom*. New York: Miller, Orton, and Mulligan, 1855. New York: Penguin Books, 2003.

Genovese, Eugene D. *Roll, Jordan, Roll: The World the Slaves Made*. New York: Pantheon Books, 1974.

Jacobs, Harriet A. *Incidents in the Life of a Slave Girl*. Boston: Published for the author, 1861. Cambridge: Harvard University Press, 1987, 2000.

Lowance, Mason, ed. *Against Slavery: An Abolitionist Reader*. New York: Penguin Books, 2000.

McFeely, William S. *Frederick Douglass*. New York: W. W. Norton, 1991.

Quarles, Benjamin. *Black Abolitionists*. New York: Oxford University Press, 1969. New York: Da Capo Press, 1991.

Stowe, Harriet Beecher. *Uncle Tom's Cabin; or, Life Among the Lowly*. Boston: John P. Jewett & Company; Cleveland: Jewett, Proctor & Worthington, 1852. New York: Oxford University Press, 2002.

Truth, Sojourner. *Narrative of Sojourner Truth*. Boston: Printed for the author, 1850. New York: Penguin Books, 1998.

Acknowledgments

All possible care has been taken to trace ownership and secure permission for each selection in this book. The Great Books Foundation wishes to thank the following authors, publishers, and representatives for permission to reprint copyrighted material:

The Trials of Girlhood, from INCIDENTS IN THE LIFE OF A SLAVE GIRL, WRITTEN BY HERSELF, by Harriet A. Jacobs, edited and with an introduction by Jean Fagen Yellin, pp. 27–30, Cambridge, Mass.: Harvard University Press. Copyright 1987, 2000 by the President and Fellows of Harvard College. Reprinted by permission of the publisher.

The Narrative *as Literature*, from FREDERICK DOUGLASS, by William S. McFeely. Copyright 1991 by William S. McFeely. Reprinted by permission of W. W. Norton & Company, Inc.

Photo and Art Credits

All possible care has been taken to trace ownership and secure permission for each image in this book. **cover** Romare Bearden, *Prevalence of Ritual Tidings* (1964). Collage of various papers with graphite on cardboard, 7.75 x 10.5 inches. Collection Stéphane Janssen, AZ. Print from the National Gallery of Art, Office of Publications, Washington, DC. © Romare Howard Bearden Foundation/Licensed by VAGA, New York, NY. **ii** National Portrait Gallery, Smithsonian Institution/Art Resource, NY. **10** The Granger Collection, NY. **12** The Maryland State Archives. **14** Chester County Historical Society, West Chester, PA. **15** Courtesy of the Library of Congress. **16** National Park Service, Frederick Douglass National Historic Site. **19** Photo by Ezra Greenleaf Weld. The J. Paul Getty Museum, Los Angeles, CA. **20** Peabody Museum of Archaeology and Ethnology, Harvard University. **25** © Bettmann/CORBIS. **33** Courtesy of the Library of Congress. **36** Courtesy of the Moorland-Springarn Research Center, Howard University. **68** Courtesy of the U.S. Army Military Historical Institute. **70** Courtesy of the Library of Congress. **75** Bruce Family Papers (#2692), Special Collections, University of Virginia Library. **76** Abby Aldrich Rockefeller Folk Art Museum, Colonial Williamsburg Foundation, Williamsburg, VA. **78** Aaron Douglas, *On de No'thern Road* (1926). From *Opportunity* magazine. © National Urban League. **79** Aaron Douglas, *I couldn't hear nobody pray* (1925). From *Opportunity* magazine. © National Urban League. **80** Aaron Douglas, *Forest Fear* (1926). Private collection. **83** Romare Bearden, *Watching the Good Trains Go By* (1964). Collage of various papers with graphite on cardboard, 13.75 x 16.875 inches. Courtesy of the collection of Philip J. and Suzanne Schiller, American Social Commentary Art, 1930–1970. Print from the National Gallery of Art, Office of Publications, Washington, DC. © Romare Howard Bearden Foundation/Licensed by VAGA, New York, NY. **85** Courtesy of the North Carolina Office of Archives and History, Raleigh, NC. **88** The Library Company of Philadelphia. **94** The Granger Collection, NY. **96** Virginia Historical Society, Richmond, VA. **101** Courtesy of the Library of Congress. **102** (t, l) Courtesy of the President and Fellows of Harvard College. **102** (t, r) Courtesy of the Library of Congress. **102** (b, l) American Antiquarian Society. **102** (b, r) Courtesy of the Library of Congress. **103** (t, l) © Collection of the New-York Historical Society. **103** (t, r) The Bostonian Society/Old State House. **103** (b, l) © CORBIS. **103** (b, r) Theodor Kaufmann, *On to Liberty* (1867). Oil on canvas. Private collection/Bridgeman Art Library. Christie's Images. **104** National Portrait Gallery, Smithsonian Institution/Art Resource, NY. **112** P&S-1954.0015. Chicago Historical Society. **118** © Kelly-Mooney Photography/CORBIS. **120** (t) Courtesy of the Library of Congress. **120** (b) Courtesy of the Library of Congress. **120–121** Courtesy of the Library of Congress. **121** (t) © CORBIS. **121** (b) The Granger Collection, NY. **122** William Townsend, *Marqu*. Beinecke Rare Book and Manuscript Library, Yale University. **124** William Townsend, *Fuli*. Beinecke Rare Book and Manuscript Library, Yale University. **125** William Townsend, *Little Kale*. Beinecke Rare Book and Manuscript Library, Yale University. **126** Lezley Saar, *Harriet Hemmings, Slave Daughter of Thomas Jefferson* (1999). Mixed media, 80 x 48 x 4 inches. © Lezley Saar. **136** Photo by Alexander Gardner. ICHi-11439. Chicago Historical Society. **139** © Collection of the New-York Historical Society.